SoJourn
Volume 3, Number 2

A journal devoted to the history, culture, and geography of South Jersey

Winter 2018–2019

SoJourn is a collaborative effort. Local historians contribute the articles; Stockton students—in this issue, the editing interns of fall 2018—edit the articles, set the type, and design the layout; the directors of the South Jersey Culture & History Center at Stockton University oversee the publication.

Editors
Kelly Burns, Angela Capella, Joshua Champlin, Daniel Cordero, Bradford Cress, Jessica English, Brendan Helm, Sarah Holt, Haylee Korbobo, Alexandra Llerena, Jessica A. Lyon, Claire Riley, Kailey Romero, Gabriela Siwiec, Shannon Stolz and Pablo Tavarez.

Supervising Editors
Tom Kinsella and Paul W. Schopp

ISSN: 2474-6665
ISBN-13: 978-1-947889-93-4
A publication of the South Jersey Culture & History Center
at Stockton University
www.stockton.edu/sjchc/

© 2019, the authors, South Jersey Culture & History Center, and Stockton University. All rights reserved.

Filler images, at the conclusion of articles, courtesy of the Paul W. Schopp Collection unless otherwise noted.

To contact SJCHC write:
SJCHC / School of Arts & Humanities
Stockton University
101 Vera King Farris Drive
Galloway, New Jersey
08205

Email:
Thomas.Kinsella@stockton.edu
Paul.Schopp@stockton.edu

About this Issue of *SoJourn*

Welcome to the sixth issue of *SoJourn*, a twice-yearly journal chronicling the history, culture and geography of southern New Jersey. Here are eleven articles describing events in localities stretching from Camden to Absecon, and from Camp Dix to Port Norris, along with points in between. The events described date from the seventeenth century, through the nineteenth century, World War I, and to very recent history.

Our lead article, "The Southern Pine Barrens: An Ethnic Archipelago," updates an important essay, first published in 1979, describing the impact of geography upon patterns of settlement in the Pine Barrens below the Mullica River. Another article describes a spectacular South Jersey crime story which captivated the nation in the early 1930s. Still another presents the romanticized, mid-nineteenth-century version of the founding of Haddonfield. Along the way, you will read about horseshoe crabs, Jewish farming communities, folk music, and more.

We are proud of the quality of work that we continue to offer to readers. Stockton University editing interns provide attractive editing, layout, and design for each issue. Authors contribute excellent articles. We encourage those of you with pertinent articles or stories to contact the *SoJourn* editors so that future issues will include your work, providing new details on the rich cultural heritage of South Jersey.

       Tom Kinsella

       Director
       South Jersey Culture & History Center
       Stockton University

MAP OF CONTENTS

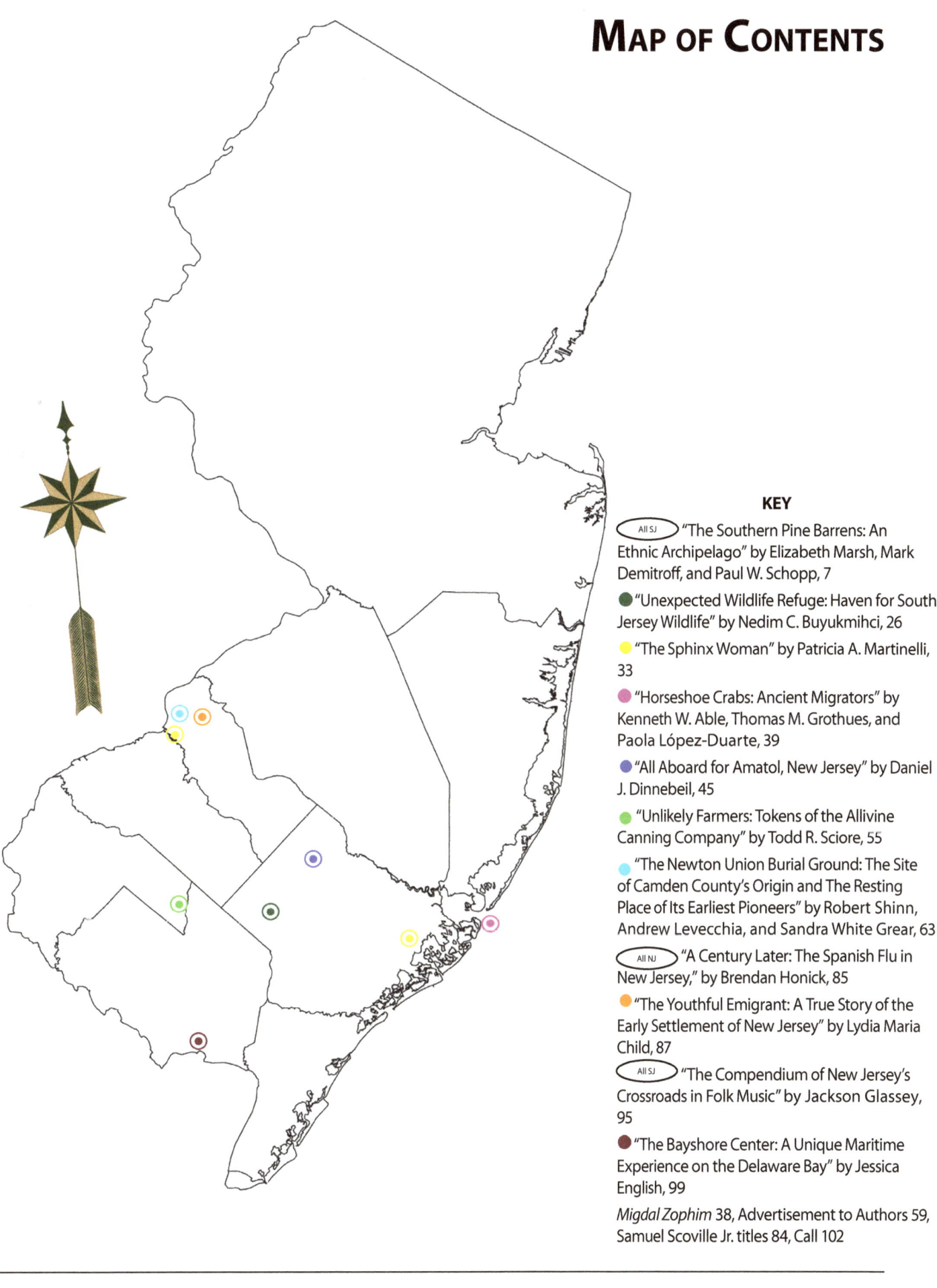

KEY

- (All SJ) "The Southern Pine Barrens: An Ethnic Archipelago" by Elizabeth Marsh, Mark Demitroff, and Paul W. Schopp, 7
- ● "Unexpected Wildlife Refuge: Haven for South Jersey Wildlife" by Nedim C. Buyukmihci, 26
- ● "The Sphinx Woman" by Patricia A. Martinelli, 33
- ● "Horseshoe Crabs: Ancient Migrators" by Kenneth W. Able, Thomas M. Grothues, and Paola López-Duarte, 39
- ● "All Aboard for Amatol, New Jersey" by Daniel J. Dinnebeil, 45
- ● "Unlikely Farmers: Tokens of the Allivine Canning Company" by Todd R. Sciore, 55
- ● "The Newton Union Burial Ground: The Site of Camden County's Origin and The Resting Place of Its Earliest Pioneers" by Robert Shinn, Andrew Levecchia, and Sandra White Grear, 63
- (All NJ) "A Century Later: The Spanish Flu in New Jersey," by Brendan Honick, 85
- ● "The Youthful Emigrant: A True Story of the Early Settlement of New Jersey" by Lydia Maria Child, 87
- (All SJ) "The Compendium of New Jersey's Crossroads in Folk Music" by Jackson Glassey, 95
- ● "The Bayshore Center: A Unique Maritime Experience on the Delaware Bay" by Jessica English, 99

Migdal Zophim 38, Advertisement to Authors 59, Samuel Scoville Jr. titles 84, Call 102

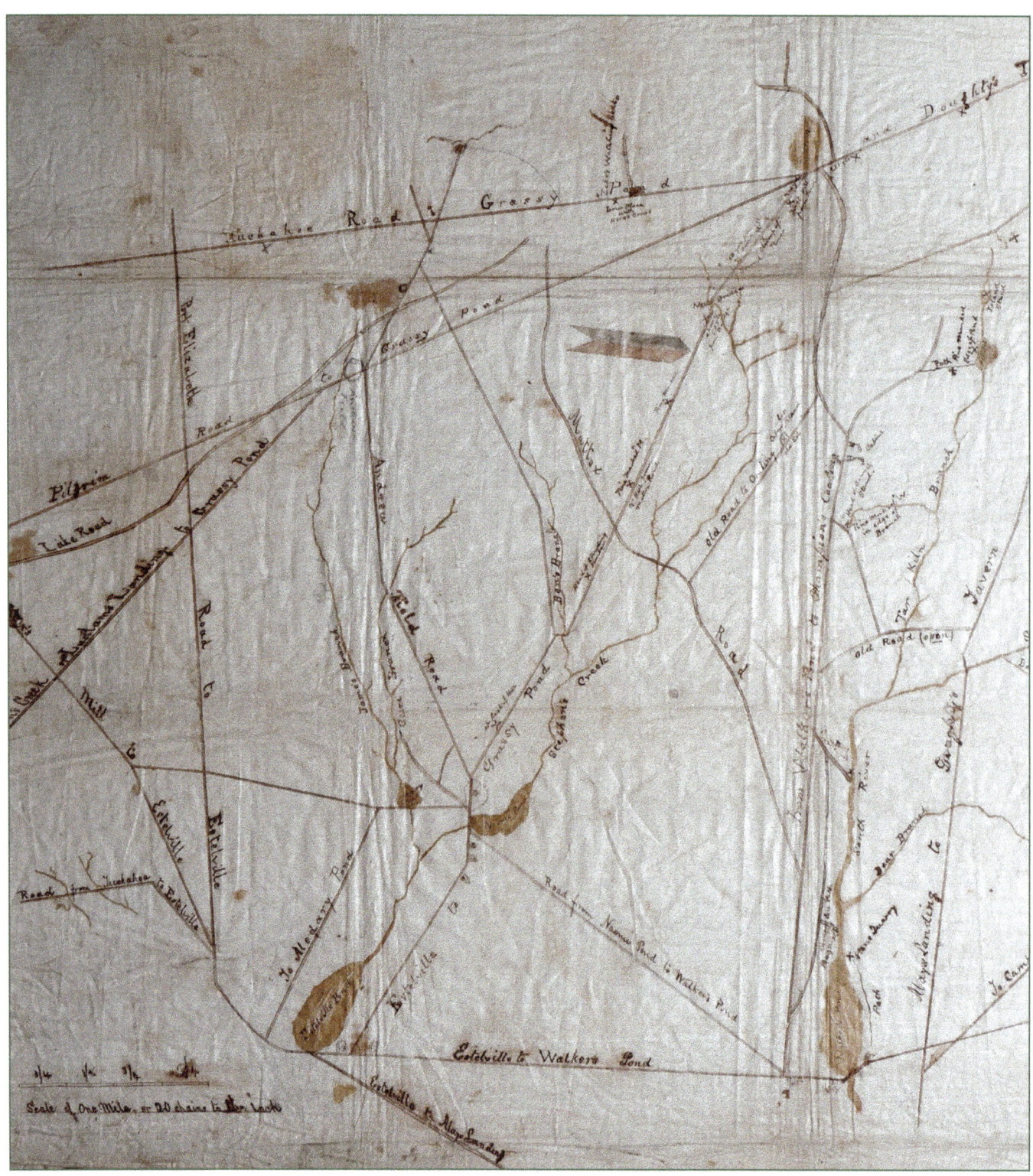

Detail from the Willits Estelville-Port Elizabeth Map. Drawn on linen by Dr. Reuben Willits, dated approximately to 1830, this large map was acquired from the estate of Willits' descendent, J. Howard Willits McAllister. In February 1826, Willits, originally of Cape May, wed Hannah Elfreth Brick, the daughter of a family that had Bricksboro platted. Her grandfather, Joshua Brick Sr., served as a delegate to the Continental Congress session held in Bridgeton on December 22, 1774. In 1814, upon the death of James Lee, Joshua came into ownership of Port Elizabeth's best known industry, the Eagle Glass Works, which produced window glass. Joshua held the manufactory for a time before conveying it to Samuel P. Wetherill in 1818. Married after the death of Hannah's first husband, Dr. Benjamin Fisler, also a Port Elizabeth resident, the Willitses settled in the Brick residence on Broadway in Port Elizabeth. The couple had four children. This map and other family heirlooms descended to Willits' daughter, Carolyn, the wife of one-time U.S. Senator Albert Robeson McAllister, and then to their son, J. Howard. The map depicts several landmarks still identifiable today, notably, the road from Mays Landing to Doughty's Tavern and Millville, which is now County Route 552. The community of Milmay is located at the intersection of Pilgrim Road and Grassy Pond, now Route 557. The road diverging from it, Tuckahoe Road to Grassy Pond, also still exists, running into Route 548. This map, originally donated to the Cumberland County Historical Society, has recently been turned over to Special Collections of the Bjork Library at Stockton University, where it augments the Estell-Bourgeois Collection.

The Southern Pine Barrens:
An Ethnic Archipelago

Elizabeth Marsh, Mark Demitroff, and Paul W. Schopp

An unusual distribution pattern of railroad-era ethnic settlement in New Jersey's southern interior can be explained through regional human-environmental relationships. Although geographers often find it difficult to humanize the physical elements of a place, the diverse physical substrate (the lay-of-the-land) of the southern Pine Barrens afforded exploitation opportunity to Eastern and Southern European immigrants. A two-part argument is presented here, bridging the geographic divide between physical and cultural dynamics, respectively. A mosaic of wet lowlands and droughty uplands, characteristic of the southern Pine Barrens, created conditions for the development of a highly distinctive "ethnic archipelago" of farms, industries, and habitations during the late nineteenth and early twentieth centuries.

The "southern Pine Barrens," that part of the New Jersey Outer Coastal Plain[1] lying below the Mullica River, lacks the mystery of its counterpart, the Wharton Tract, and its endless pine woods in Burlington and Ocean Counties. The forest below the Mullica, although expansive, no longer supports stands of pygmy pines, and its indigenous population of reclusive Pineys declined at a date earlier than its complement above the Mullica.[2] Instead, the southern Pine Belt appears as a flat, prosaic plain; and, in its cultural appearance, it is part-and-parcel an element of standard small-town rural America. Furthermore, the southern Pines are not even particularly piney or barren; the slightly richer soil supports some agriculture and the woods often comprise more oak than pine.[3]

The intent of this article is to first recognize and then celebrate the southern Pine Barrens to foster its study.[4] The text below draws attention to two geographic aspects: 1) this region in landform is an upland archipelago of fast-land islands and peninsulas located among vast wet lowlands of the interior;[5] and 2) those uplands were droughty and infertile, being of meager agricultural value to early settlers.[6] It was only with the great migrations during the railroad era that portions of this land became densely settled (see fig. 2 on the following page).

Only two or three generations have passed since this land became agriculturally viable, and, in-part, continues today as a loose patchwork of immigrant ethnic settlements.[7] A review of the relevant plates

Figure 1. LiDAR image map of New Jersey Pine Barrens including outliers as defined by McCormick & Andresen (1963)—sandy land where pines predominate and which has been historically unsuitable (barren) for agricultural production. Adapted from image provided by Boyd Ostroff, "The Art of Mapmaking," https://boydsmaps.com.

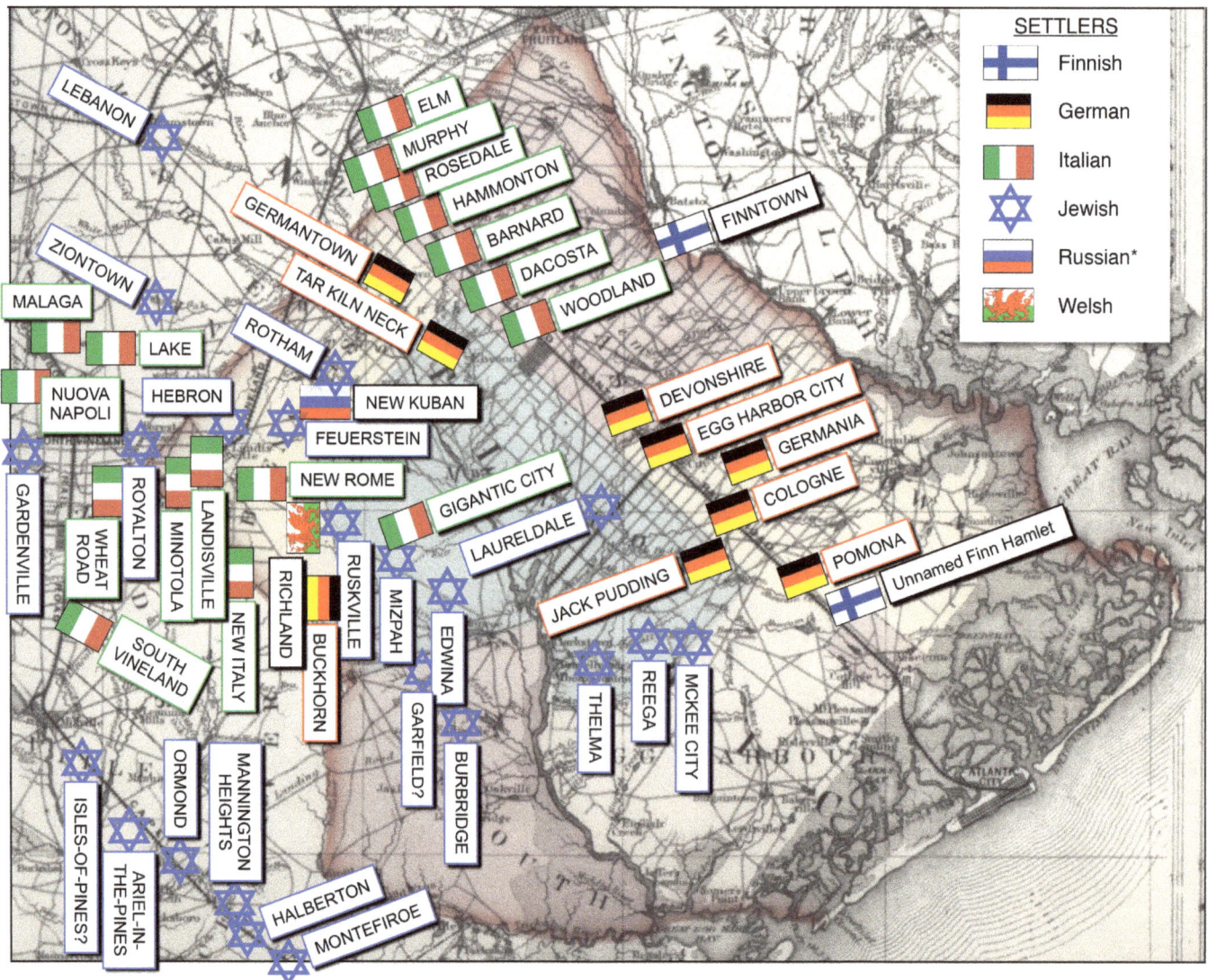

Figure 2. Ethnic settlements in the southern Pine Barrens. The southern Pine Barrens is here defined as the area delineated as "Pine Barrens" by McCormick & Andresen (1963) that is below the course of the Mullica River, starting at the river's headwaters proximate to Medford and continuing eastward down to its mouth near Leeds Point. The Jewish colonies of Alliance, Rosenhayn, and Carmel, while having much in common with the settlements here identified, are technically outside of the Pine Barrens, and thus not shown.

covering the southern Pine Barrens from Cook and Vermeule's historic and topographic *New Jersey Atlas Sheets*[8] reveals that the railroads, and the road builders before them, used these interior fast-land islands and peninsulas as rights-of-way in an early cultural adaptation of the physical landscape. By "reading" the landforms and their proximate relationship, it allowed, as much as possible, the surveyors charged with laying out the routes to avoid the surrounding swampy wetlands and the attendant expenses of constructing causeways, cribbing, culverts, trestles, and bridges.

The Archipelago[9]

The southern Pine Barrens extend from the headwaters of the Mullica River at Medford, down to Leeds Point (above Atlantic City), and over to the Delaware Bay—including Cape May County to the latitude of Stone Harbor. Based on topographic mapping, this territory appears to comprise terra firma, but a casual pedestrian exploration demonstrates that vast portions of the interior are inundated with water for at least part of the year. In Atlantic County, about 28 percent of the mainland is classified as wetland-related "hydric"[10] soil: e.g., Atsion, Berryland, Muck, and Mullica.[11]

These interior swamps, in an unusual configuration, tend to form as inland features associated with the headwaters of Pine Barrens streams. PaleoIndians, the earliest aboriginals, employed foraging economies based on ephemeral episodes of faunal procurement at camps associated with Ice Age-generated wetlands and dunes. Later precontact cultures engaged in a more diverse

An Ethnic Archipelago

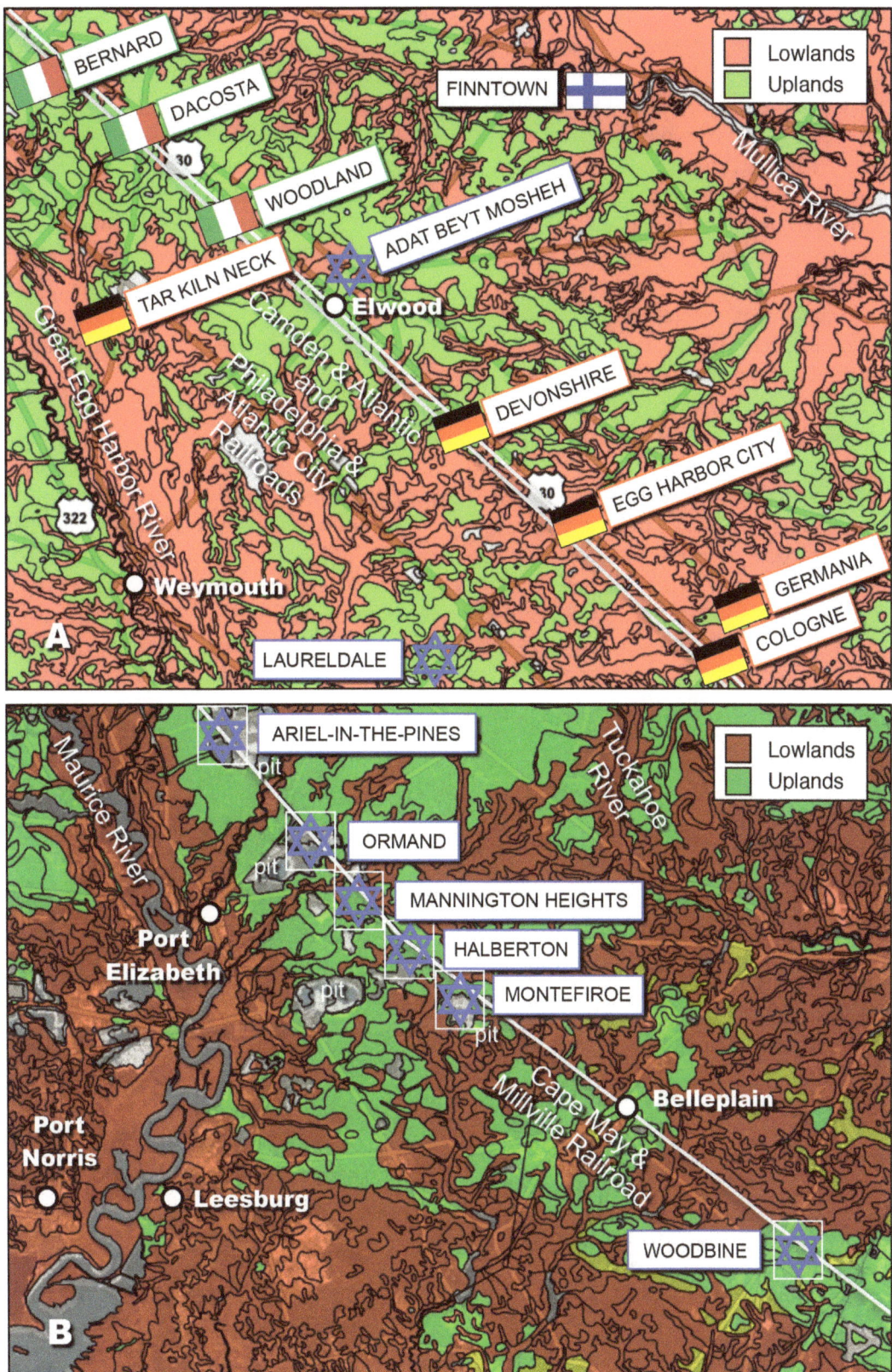

Figure 3. Soils maps indicating high ground (in green) where dwellings with basements can be built and lower ground (in red) where depth to water table, ponding, and/or flooding limits the building of dwellings with basements. A. Ethnic hamlets in northern Atlantic County, primarily clustered along the railroad lines. B. Ethnic hamlets along a railroad line near the intersection of Atlantic, Cape May, and Cumberland Counties. Note an abundance of gravel pit operations today (in white) using the pebbly capping of relict plateau where ventures failed. Adapted from Soil Survey Staff, Natural Resources Conservation Service, United States Department of Agriculture. Web Soil Survey. Available online at the following link: https://websoilsurvey.sc.egov.usda.gov/.

range of seasonal-round activities at these same Ice Age landforms, last of which were the Lenape.[12] Pioneer European settlers sought the land-use capabilities of the highest, driest lands along the coast and riverbanks during the earliest occupation period. In advance of the "Ethnic Archipelago" settlement model, the raised islands of upland, known as relict plateaus, rim the coastland and divide river courses as high ground interfluve,[13] rising above an impassible network of broad planar swampland. These islands provided the ethnic settlers arriving in the mid-nineteenth century with land for community development (Fig. 2).

The broad inland swamps that flank Pine Barrens waterways and their headwaters are, in essence, relict drainageways associated with periglacial (cold, nonglacial) conditions in this area that characterized the Ice Age or Pleistocene epoch.[14] Much of the southern Pine Barrens land is overall flatter and at a more attenuated incline than its counterpart above the Mullica River. The general land elevation below the Mullica is lower, too, being, on average, less than 100 feet high even 30 miles inland.[15] The highest point in Atlantic County is 147 feet in Hammonton.[16] Ocean County's highest point is 231 feet[17] in a section of serial escarpments. Apple Pie Hill (Burlington County) near Chatsworth is 205 feet.[18] All are relict plateau.

Southern Pine Barrens land is flat, but beneath that land, the shallow groundwater of the Cohansey Aquifer lies in a large mound. As the Atlantic sea level rose in response to climate amelioration with the Pleistocene's end, so, too, rose groundwater levels in the Pine Barrens. In many places, fluvial (river) and eolian (wind) activity has, over the millennia, interacted with the ground surface to create low areas. Rising groundwater, due to warming temperature and sea-level rise since the Ice Age, now fills these incisions and etchings, accounting for the extant of inland swamps.[19]

Further, very little meteoric water run-off (rain, snow, etc.) traverses the sandy-soiled surface to enter adjoining streams or wetlands. Instead, most of the precipitation quickly infiltrates the porous ground and trickles into the various waterways as groundwater seep. In other flat regions, stream headwaters often begin as a series of surface rills and gullies. This is not the case in the southern

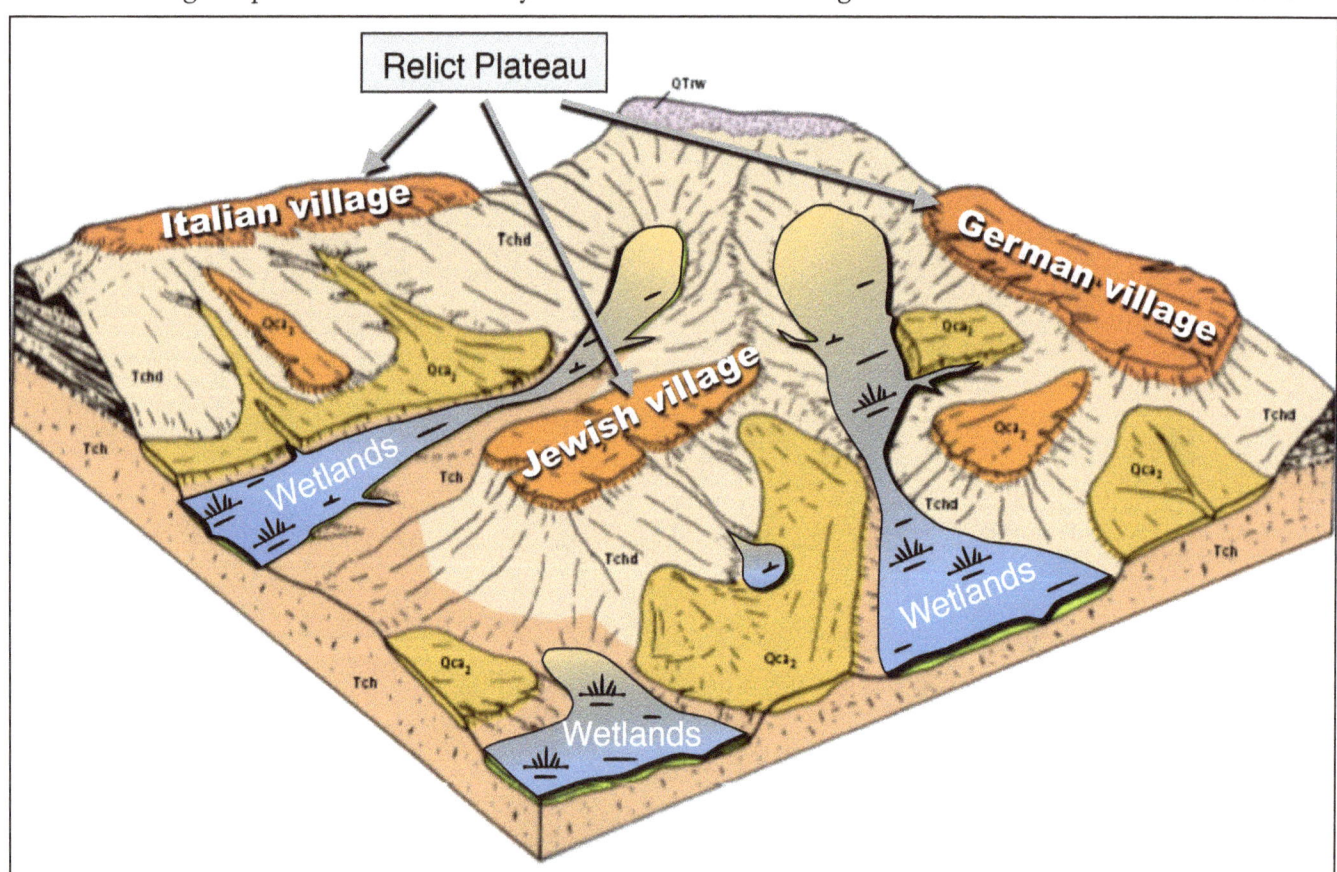

Figure 4. Archipelago model of southern Pine Barrens ethnic settlement atop higher and drier relict plateau that is surrounded by wetter lowlands. Pine Barrens high points began as old (Miocene age) river bottoms. In places where streams changed their course, gravels were deposited. In places where water flow was sluggish and swampy, ironstone formed. As those rivers changed course the abandoned channel floors became hardened caps that were more resistant to erosion than the softer old riverbanks. This is called inverted relief. Wearing away of the landscape—denudation—occurred over a very long time, with a significant amount of slope modification taking place at the end of permafrost episodes during the Ice Age.[20]

Pine Barrens. Here, the stream heads appear as groundwater-fed depressional wetlands in association with a series of closed basins known colloquially as spungs[21] and open-end dry valleys called cripples.[22] These features are artifacts derived from wind- and water-action during cold, dry, and windy periods of the Pleistocene, with some modification by the thawing of ice (thermokarst) in frozen ground.[23]

Land modification through the aggregation and degradation of permafrost under rigorous cold, dry, and windy conditions, accompanied by periglacial mass wasting, formed a badlands landscape, which laid the foundation for a distinctive southern Pine Barrens, readily adaptable as an ethnic archipelago.[24]

Ethnic Pioneers and Human Ecology[25]

What could the first European settlers do to make the southern Pines landscape and ecosystem personally or commercially viable for subsistence and/or market-based production? In practice, little, except for the aforementioned uplands along the coast and riverbanks.[26] The interior of the southern Pines held little attraction except for the vast lowland tracts of Atlantic white-cedar to the earliest immigrants—the Dutch, Swedes, English, Scots, and French—who arrived in the area after John Fenwick, an English Quaker, settled Salem in 1674. From the earliest English settlement, the pine trees yielded limited quantities of naval stores and charcoal for merchants and laborers, but a more substantial exploitation of Pine Barrens resources would not occur until another 75 years had elapsed.[27] While bog iron provided a crucial ingredient for manufacturing small cast and forged iron fittings for shipbuilding in the first half of the eighteenth century, the vast bog iron industry began ten years before the American War for Independence commenced. Soon, numerous furnaces and forges were operating, each requiring large tracts of woodland in South Jersey for charcoal production and river-terrace meadow called "savannah"[28] for ore mining.

As the iron industry faded in the mid-nineteenth century, glass manufacturing became the preeminent industry, with some of the glasshouses holding their own timberlands for fuelwood production and glass sand mining. As these industrial enterprises closed, the associated large parcels of land fell into disuse and their owners sought a new purpose for these southern Pine Barrens tracts to recoup a final financial return. Speculators and developers acquired large swaths of this land, seeking to create self-sufficient residential communities in response to the wave of immigration that began in the mid-nineteenth century and continued into the twentieth century. With railroads beginning to penetrate South Jersey by the 1850s, these large parcels of vacant south Pine Barrens land, so temptingly convenient to America's Atlantic ports of entry, provided settlement areas for the various ethnic groups arriving from Europe.

During the 1850s, three factors contributed to a new availability of this land for settlement:

1. the iron industry and its attendant ventures entered a terminal decline, rendering the extensive landholdings accumulated for charcoaling surplus and salable;[29]
2. the coming of the railroads, making the interior accessible to urban centers and moving immigrants to these new settlement areas;[30]
3. meager land became arable when soil amendments could be efficiently introduced (manures, marl,[31] fertilizers).

Abandoned Iron Furnace. Printed originally from a glass plate negative, various past local historians have identified this image of an abandoned and deteriorating Pine Barrens bog iron facility as either Hanover Furnace or Speedwell Furnace. The latter furnace is likely the correct identification.

The last-named soil amendment—commercial fertilizers[32]—came into general use following the Civil War, as did the larger irrigation pumps[33] needed for wetting the droughty sand. Correspondingly, new and often perishable crops could now be expedited out of the southern Pines due to the availability of rapid rail transportation. The ability to improve the soil for crop production, and the identification of crops suitable for commercial production in the soil, provided the settlers with a strong sense of sustainability for their families and for the community.[34]

The New Jersey Pine Barrens, situated in close proximity to three of America's largest cities, was one of the few remaining places in the East where one could still find grandchildren and even children of the pioneers, old men and women whose parents first grubbed stumps and cleared virgin land into the beginning of the twentieth century. The infertile environment initially proved so miserable, however, that no homesteader could make his way alone in the sense of the romanticized American pioneer tradition. The first settlers had to have help. Therefore, in reviewing the history of immigrant settlement in South Jersey,[35] one observes a sequential occupation in which groups with institutional (financial) support opened the land—Germans,[36] New Englanders,[37] Italians,[38] Jews,[39] and even Cossacks.[40] Each community of original inhabitants, as they climbed the economic ladder, was joined or replaced with populations holding fewer resources, a sequence in economy that continues to this day. The first wave of European settlers to tame the south Pine Barrens wilds were Germanic woodsmen, who founded Germantown or New Germany (now Folsom) on the Long-a-Coming stage route in c. 1848.[41] These Germans, many skilled laborers, were escaping the long-term turmoil associated with the aftermath of the 1848 revolutions in Prussia.[42] The first rail route to cross the southern Pines was the Camden & Atlantic Railroad (1854) and the Germans flocked to the newfound agricultural land surrounding the line.[43] The location and long-term economic success

Birds Eye View of Egg Harbor City, New Jersey. F. Scheu produced this lithographed and colorized bird's eye view of Egg Harbor City in 1865. The print depicts the community's growth since its founding less than ten years earlier. The Camden & Atlantic Railroad can be viewed in the foreground with the largest houses and factories paralleling the railroad. The escaping smoke on the extreme left side of the print is coming from a steam-powered sawmill, cutting wood to construct new houses and commercial buildings for the burgeoning city.

of these ethnic colonies depended heavily on the recent rail lines that opened new lands in support of real estate speculation and ethnic colonization.

Vineland's Charles K. Landis, born in Philadelphia to a family of Swiss origin, began his first real estate venture in 1854 on the Weymouth Tract at Colwell or Colville (now Elwood), a large town center to be surrounded by German farm-lot tracts like Germantown (now Folsom and Newtonville).[44] In 1857, Landis brought Yankee (New York and New England) gentry to Hammonton as pioneer stock; he employed German immigrants as a cheap labor pool as his first venture stalled,[45] mired in controversy and charges of financial improprieties.[46] Ultimately successful, Hammonton did not experience the growth rate of Vineland, which Landis founded in 1861.[47] Elwood never really recovered from its early fiscal scandals.[48]

Landis experienced his greatest real estate success with the founding of his utopian Vineland Colony in 1861.[49] With the onset of the Civil War, farm commodities became scarce, creating turmoil and speculative adventures for those astute enough to seize the moment. The new lands that Landis offered provided Yankee entrepreneurs from upstate New York and New England unbounded opportunities and profits from high prices attributed to crop shortages associated with wartime unrest.[50] Before the Millville & Glassboro Railroad completed its line between its two namesakes in October 1860, Vineland's population was estimated at 50 residents. By 1868, approximately 7,000 settlers called that same tract home.[51]

The arrival of the Germans and the Camden & Atlantic Railroad's presence spawned middle-class, railroad-associated, German settlements, including the Gloucester Farm and Town Association and its new town of Pomona (1854),[52] Egg Harbor City (1856),[53] and the two rural communities of Cologne and Germania that developed as outgrowths of the GFTA and Egg Harbor City settlements.[54]

The Crucial Railroads

Eight railroad companies that constructed their rail lines between 1854 and 1880 provided the impetus to develop the empty land that comprise the "islands" of the ethnic archipelago. The railroads offered a convenient and rapid way to move the émigrés to the sites of their new communities. Over time, the ownership of these lines fell to the Pennsylvania Railroad (rows 1 through 5 in the Table 1, below, between 1871 and 1883) and the Central Railroad of New Jersey (rows 6 and 7 in Table 1, gained control in 1878). Beginning in 1883, the Philadelphia & Reading Railroad also owned rail lines in South Jersey, including the Philadelphia & Atlantic City Railroad and its subsidiaries, but these lines did not materially contribute to the initial development of ethnic settlements within the archipelago except row 8, the second route to Cape May, of which the Philadelphia & Reading became the full operator in 1898 and the owner in 1901.

The network of southern Pine Barrens rail lines continued to grow during the late nineteenth century, providing access to cheap, albeit poor, land at a time when Russian pogroms were driving Jews out of Russia, beginning in 1881. Wealthy benefactors and philanthropists in Western Europe, sympathetic to their Eastern European brethren's plight, provided resettlement funds for those who could escape the persecution. Some Jewish colonies—inspired by religious motivation through these benefactors—are well known, including places like Alliance, Rosenhayn, Carmel, and Woodbine.[55] Many more Jewish settlements, however, motivated more by pecuniary return and commercial speculation, and less supported by philanthropic funding, remain enigmatic, e.g., Burbridge Village, Lebanon, and Ruskville.[56] The success of the early Jewish colonies—primarily on better lands west of Vineland—ushered in a railroad-era speculative boom across the poorer soils to the east of Vineland. The Panic of 1893 doomed the latter poorly funded

The Vineland Railway's locomotive Cumberland, pulling the first revenue train, prepares to leave Vineland on the morning of August 9, 1871, with coaches borrowed from the New Jersey Southern Railway. The train operated as part of Vineland's tenth anniversary and ran to Atsion. Charles K. Landis, desirous of having direct rail service between Vineland and the immigration nexus of New York City, obtained a legislative charter for the Vineland Railway in March 1867. Photograph courtesy of the Paul W. Schopp collection.

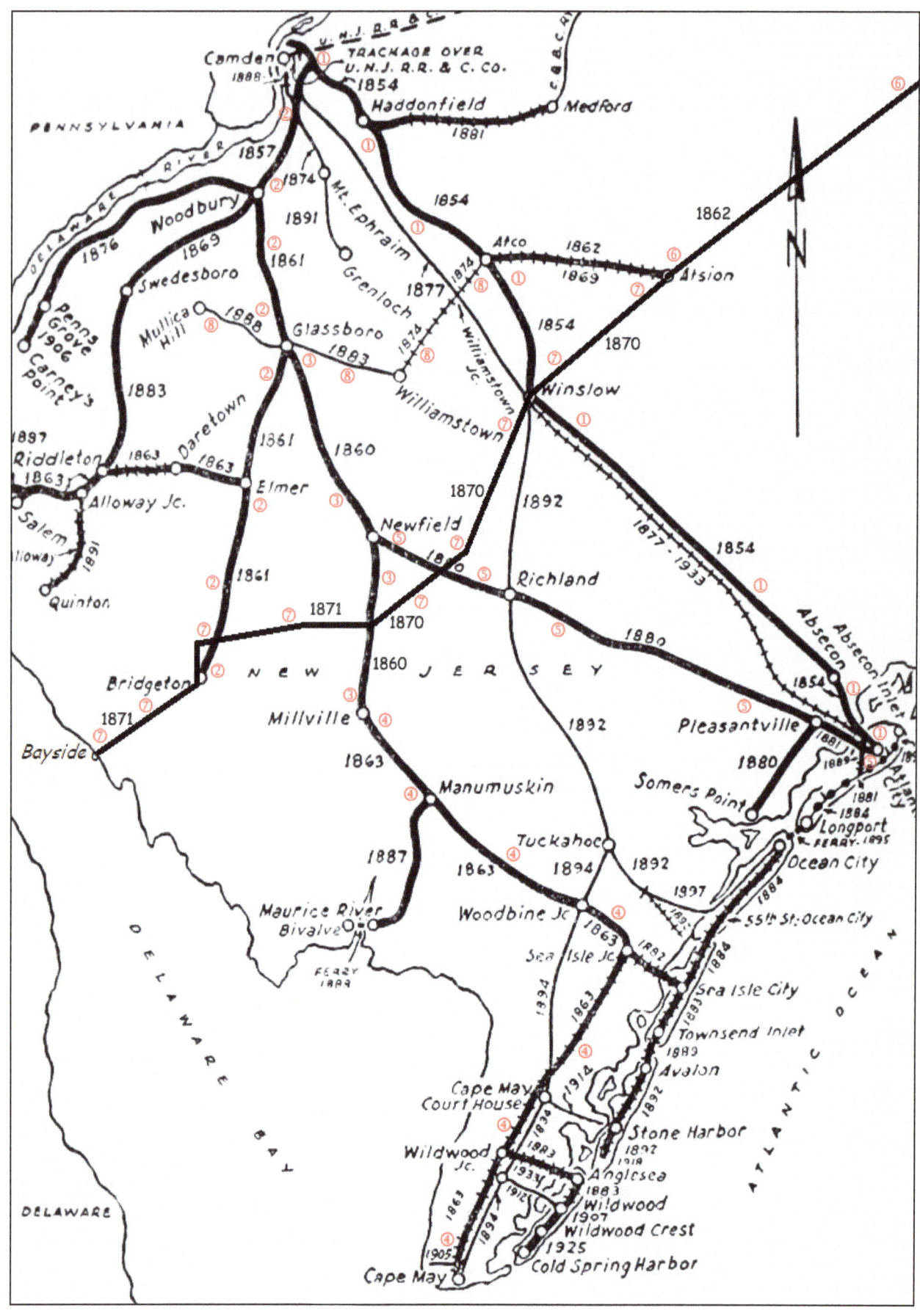

Figure 5. Annotated Map of South Jersey Railroads[57]

An Ethnic Archipelago

Table 1. Railroads that Aided Ethnic Community Development					
No. on Map	Railroad Name	Formed	Finished	North Terminus	South Terminus
1	Camden & Atlantic Railroad	1852	1854	Camden	Atlantic City
2	West Jersey Railroad	1853	1863	Camden	Bridgeton
3	Millville & Glassboro Railroad	1859	1860	Glassboro	Millville
4	Cape May & Millville Railroad	1863	1863	Millville	Cape May
5	West Jersey & Atlantic Railroad	1879	1880	Newfield	Atlantic City
6	Raritan & Delaware Bay Railroad	1854	1862	Port Monmouth	Atsion
7	Vineland Railway	1867	1871	Atsion	Bayside
8	South Jersey Railroad	1893	1894	Winslow Junction	Cape May

Table 2. The Railroads and the Associated Ethnic Communities		
No. on Map	Railroad Name	Community Names (North–South)
1	Camden & Atlantic Railroad	Atco (G), Murphy (I), Rosedale (I), Bellhurst (I), Hammonton, Da Costa (I), Elwood, Egg Harbor City (G), Germania (G), Cologne (G), Pomona (G)
2	West Jersey Railroad	Connected Philadelphia/Camden to the Millville & Glassboro at Glassboro
3	Millville & Glassboro Railroad	Malaga (I), Gardenville (J). Clayville (I), Vineland, South Vineland (I)
4	Cape May & Millville Railroad	Ariel-in-the-Pines/Sons of Israel (J), Mannington Heights (J), Ormond (J), Montefiroe (J), Halberton (J), Woodbine (J)
5	West Jersey & Atlantic Railroad	Royalton (J), Buena (I), New Rome (I), Richland (Welsh) Ruskville (J), Mizpah (J), Edwina (J), Thelma (J), Reega (J).
6	Raritan & Delaware Bay Railroad	Connected New York City to Vineland Railway at Atsion (Fruitland) (I)
7	Vineland Railway	Hebron (J), Landisville (I), Minotola (I), Wheat Road (I), Vineland, Norma (J), Rosenhayn (J), Garton (J), Brotmanville (J), Alliance (J), Carmel (J)
8	South Jersey Railroad	Folsom (G), Rotham (J)
Key Codes: (G)=German; (I)=Italian; (J)=Jewish		

colonies. Some of their time-ravaged remnants still lie along now abandoned rail routes like the West Jersey & Atlantic Railroad—but most are lost to oblivion.[58]

With the establishment of the various ethnic communities, a pattern of sequential occupation recurs.[59] Through technological innovation, the foundational Yankee settlers, and then their German counterparts, prospered. Italian recruits arrived to perform farm labor and railroad work. Northern Italians came to tend the vineyards of Vineland and Galloway Township, the latter in support of

Egg Harbor City. Southern Italians began arriving in Hammonton during the late 1860s, but emigration rose sharply when local Germans failed to provide the necessary labor for the 1877 harvest.[60] These Italian emigrants arrived exclusively from just two areas—the village of Gesso, Sicily, and from Salerno, in southwestern Italy. As an example of sequential occupation, as the Italians made economic and lifestyle gains, Latin Americans arrived to fill the labor niche that the Germans first occupied and then the Italians. By the mid-twentieth century, Puerto Ricans were the earliest Spanish-speaking arrivals to work the fields,[61] now supplanted by the Mexicans and Creole-speaking Haitians as the necessary agrarian labor force.[62]

A different, lesser-known, economic sequencing occurred ancillary to the South Jersey Jewish colonies, which became rural population centers when Ashkenazi Jews arrived from Eastern Europe (e.g., Ukraine, Russia, Poland).[63] In places, non-Hebrew Ukrainians either intermingled or were bracketed with Eastern European Jews. Many of these Christians remained in the Pines, even as their Jewish counterparts relocated for new opportunities in urban centers—some earning higher educational degrees, which Jewish aid societies subsidized.[64] Concurrently, urban blacks replaced the outgoing Jews in this succession at places like Mizpah, McKee City, and Woodbine. Many people of color had left the South during the First World War to take factory jobs, only to be ousted when veterans returned at war's end. Rather than return South, they, too, found solitude and security on Pinelands homesteads.[65]

Ethnic colonization continued through the twentieth century. Displaced people (DPs), such as Jewish survivors

Weintrob family gathering in Thelma, New Jersey, c.1902. The isolated farmstead was purchased in 1898, and remained in production for about a decade. While the hamlet itself was not explicitly a Jewish construct, geographical proximity to Reega played a role here—Thelma adopted Reega's West Jersey & Atlantic train station. Photograph courtesy of the Andrew Almanza collection.

with numbers tattooed on their arms, arrived during and after the war against Nazi Germany. These DPs left South Jersey a decade or two later, leaving behind now-derelict chicken coops and simple rural synagogues along southern Pine Barrens country roads (e.g., Laureldale).[66] The DPs, in turn, found themselves intermingled or replaced with yet other groups from the rim of the former Soviet Union. Monasteries and gold-domed churches can be found here and there across Cumberland and Atlantic counties, like the two still extant at the Cossack community of New Kuban.[67] In another corner of Atlantic County, a community of Finns assembled that, with some integrity, maintained its customs and ethnic identity.[68]

A more recent manifestation of these ethnic communities was represented in a small-but-cohesive, self-aware enclave of religious converts known as the "Black Jews of Elwood."[69] This community had

An Ethnic Archipelago

Mizpah Sewing Factory (top). Mizpah Agricultural and and Industrial Company ladies-wear sewing factory (c. 1891), the economic engine of a Jewish colony settled along the West Jersey & Atlantic Railroad west of Mays Landing. A speculative railroad boom around 1890 facilitated the opening of a multitude of sweatshops in the Pine Barrens, their success predicated upon cheap immigrant labor. Economic instability due to under-capitalization, exacerbated by the Panic of 1893, resulted in the rapid failure of many of these initiatives. The building is recently idle, last being used by a graphic arts company. Photograph courtesy of Sherman Hartman.

Illustrations for Southern Pine Barrens Planned Town (below).[70] Vignette adorning the bottom section of a large map: "Map No. 2 of Montefiore, Maurice River Township, Cumberland Co. N. J. Property of Cumberland Land and Improvement Co." c. 1900. Courtesy of the Cumberland County Historical Society.

maintained a presence along Route 561 since 1962, but the Adat Beyt Mosheh congregational center is now closed.[71] Looking at the wider New Jersey cultural landscape, other more recent arrivals include the Buddhist Kalmyks of Howell and Medford (Mongol Horde remnants, under Cossack protection, that first came to New Kuban),[72] along with the Gypsies of Jackson,[73] and a small Polish settlement in Absecon Highlands.[74]

New Appreciation of Southern Pine Barrens Cultural History

There are parts of America we have long recognized as sustaining important ethnic or cultural moments in history—places like Appalachia, Lancaster County, and the New York metropolitan area. To this legacy we add the southern Pine Barrens, or, better yet, the whole Pinelands National Reserve. Students of all ages should embrace and study this special center of diversity. The ethnic archipelago might be viewed as an important cultural construct and a handy tool to explore a once common heritage. Here the term "Piney" is recast to apply a multicultural designation that transcends temporal, political, religious, and ethnic/racial lines.

That South Jersey possesses a distinctive cultural landscape, including its association with the early Jewish colonies, is little known. While the more religious colonies have gained some renown, the freethinker settlements east of Vineland are all but forgotten. Classic and popular historic narratives emphasize Lenape prehistory, minor naval wartime skirmishes, and chronicle the exploits of early English and Quaker settlers, but ethnic settlement accounts are marginal in local history. Nevertheless, these "other" people who call the interior southern Pine Barrens home discuss, value, and celebrate their German, Italian, Ukrainian, or other ethnic heritage, as do the modern Jewish communities of Margate and Vineland.

It was the original intent of the first author, and the hope of her posthumous contributors, that others will also see the worthiness and importance of the southern Pine Barrens as a place of popular notice and scholarly investigation. This scope includes both the region's physical environment and the rich settlement history of those who chose to live here. In pursuit of a study, there are geographical qualities that are of particular note: 1) the recentness of settlement; 2) the physical isolation of each group on its own island in the archipelago; 3) a post-immigration continuity of European traditions, 4) how immigrants assimilate; and 5) the fleeting opportunity to record an under-valued cache of ethnic folklore and folkways—all subjects that hold scholarly promise.

Hebron Button Factory/Social Hall (bottom). Hebron Jewish colony sewing/button factory (c. 1891), an ill-fated ethnic community settled on the Jersey Central Railroad (formerly the Vineland Railway) just north of Landisville. An upstairs great hall accommodated social space for lessons, plays, and dances. With failure, its houses were moved to Landisville and the train station abandoned, although the dormitory and outbuildings remain to this day. Later, the enterprise complex became a mushroom/produce farm under Italian ownership and is currently slated for reuse through agrotourism and hydroponics.

Libby Marsh

In 1979, Elizabeth Redfield Marsh published her groundbreaking article on the cultural geography of South Jersey, "The Southern Pine Barrens: an Ethnic Archipelago."[75] Marsh, called "Libby" by her friends and colleagues at, then, Stockton State College, was an Associate Professor of Environmental Studies; she would later become the first woman promoted to full professor in the sciences at Stockton and chair of the Division of Natural Sciences and Mathematics. She details in her essay the interplay between the landscape of South Jersey and the immigrant groups who arrived to make it their home. Although influential over the succeeding years, her work has not been easily accessed or as well-known as it deserves to be. SJCHC has, accordingly, updated and republished the article, with permission. We hope that, in this revised form, it will continue to spur research and study into the rich cultural history of southern New Jersey. It remains an enduring testament to the work and memory of a remarkable woman.

Libby was born into a scientific family. Her father had been an oceanographer at Woods Hole Oceanographic Institution. She descended from a line of naturalists and medical school faculty on both sides of her family, including the first president of the American Association for the Advancement of Science.[76] Libby attended Reed College for two years during the war. After starting a family, she returned to college at Penn State where, inspired by Prof. Peirce F. Lewis, geographer of the American cultural landscape, she earned a PhD in 1972. From Lewis Libby learned to dismiss the division that most researchers draw between the natural sciences and the social sciences, and to understand landscapes as being equal parts physical and human products.

She was hired in the first cohort of faculty at the newly established Stockton University in 1971, helping to establish the Environmental Studies program and teaching there until her retirement in 1986.

Libby and her husband, Charlie, raised their family before she returned for her advanced degree, so upon her arrival at Stockton, she was considerably older than her students. Her passion and inventiveness, nevertheless, thoroughly engaged her students. Pat Nickles, a former student, writes, "On field trips, although Libby was 20, 30, or 40 years older than her students, she was the one who set the pace ... I remember a time when she showed us how to run down a steep hill sideways." Another student, Jim McCarthy, remembers that Libby encouraged students to learn through reasoning and discovery. She would present problems and ask students to present ideas, hypotheses, or solutions. Libby would usually acknowledge when a student was correct or on

(Above) Elizabeth "Libby" Marsh. In 1976, then Associate Professor of Environmental Studies, Marsh reviews a housing map that she and students prepared for the Atlantic County Planning Division. Courtesy of the Stockton *Chronicle*, November 22, 1976.

(Below) Libby in front of a display of Pine Barrens plant resources. Courtesy of the Stockton *Chronicle*, September 15, 1975.

the right path to discovery, but not always. Developing methods of analysis and discovery were more important than learning facts. "On one particular field trip," McCarthy writes, "I recall Libby brought the class to a roadway that stretched across the marshes between a mainland formation and a barrier island. She pointed to an unusual landmass, which supported a few mature trees and rose above the surrounding marshland. Libby asked, 'What caused that land mass to rise above the surrounding marsh?' Students offered their ideas, none of which received a word or glance of affirmation. After a while and without conclusion, we moved on. To this day, I still think about the forces of man or nature that might explain that land mass, but more importantly, because of Libby, I try to examine all unusual formations on land and in life thoughtfully."

A recognizable figure on campus who rode a bicycle to work, Libby was admired by her colleagues and students alike. To younger faculty in Environmental Studies, she became a mentor. To students, she was an inspiration. Nickles writes, "During the wonderful years that I knew and worked closely with her, she taught me that I too could do astonishing things."

Libby was active in the community. She worked to establish the Atlantic City Coastal Museum, serving as its co-chair when, in 1979, it re-opened Atlantic City's Absecon Lighthouse to visitors.[77] A member of the Atlantic City Area Friends Meeting, her Quaker principles shaped most aspects of how she worked, both at Stockton and in Galloway Township, where she served many years on the planning board. Jamie Cromartie, Associate Professor Emeritus of Entomology, notes that for years, while Libby was an active participant, Stockton's Environmental Studies faculty never voted on any proposal or recommendation. They always worked, often with Libby's guidance, to reach a consensus in the best Quaker tradition.

Her concerns as a teacher and a geographer always centered upon the relationship of people to the land. She took a great interest in all aspects of her field, from paleoenvironments to vernacular architecture. Cromartie recalls her ability to tell in what decade a house had been built from the details of its design. People, however, remained her central focus. After she retired, she and Charlie lived in Lewisburg, Pennsylvania, where she devoted much of her time to the Lewisburg Prison Project, helping many who had no other friends and very little hope.

John Sinton, Professor Emeritus of Environmental Studies, provides a description of Libby's character and of a formative moment for the creation of the accompanying article:

> What a vortex of energy she was! Hawk-like, Libby would pierce any presumption or supercilious comment and pick at empty arguments until she finished whatever task she had started. She and I shared an aggrieved

Walking the Marsh. Elizabeth "Libby" Marsh in her element, with (from left to right) Stockton professors Ralph Bean and Al Steinberg and Dean Dan Moury. This image, without caption, was used to illustrate the *Stockton State Prospectus 72*.

sense of injustice in the world, which led her to study the poor people and hidden residents in South Jersey—thus her pursuit of the various immigrant groups in the Pine Barrens. As she waded into the research, she called me into the office on a Friday and fairly shouted, "I've got it! This place is an ETHNIC ARCHIPELAGO!

Libby Marsh died on October 9, 2009. Her students, friends, and colleagues still miss her.

This brief review of the life of Elizabeth Redfield Marsh was prepared from descriptions and comments provided by Dick Colby, Jamie Cromartie, Claude Epstein, Alice Gitchell, Jim McCarthy, Pat Nickles, and John Sinton

About the Authors

Demitroff is a 'native' Pinelands natural historian and licensed tree expert who internationally publishes and lectures on local geography—notably Pleistocene past permafrost. He received a BS in Agricultural Sciences (Rutgers University). In mid-life Mark returned to academia and won a competitive fellowship at the University of Delaware to receive an MS in Geography, then completed coursework towards a PhD in Land-Surface Processes. Mark is an adjunct instructor at Stockton University, an inaugural board member at SJCHC, and is a member of the Executive Board at the US Permafrost Association.

Paul W. Schopp is the assistant director of the South Jersey Culture & History Center at Stockton University. During his 44 years working as a local historian, Paul has acquired a heightened knowledge of South Jersey's cultural and physical landscape. Whether discussing area railroads or the various communities they served, Paul feels right at home offering his unique insights into such topics, based on his extensive research into these subjects. As coauthor of *The Trail of the Blue Comet: a History of the New Jersey Central's Southern Division*, and a number of other published works, Paul always strives for the highest hallmark of scholarship.

Acknowledgements:

We would like to thank Ben Marsh for his review, and Carl Farrell and Robert Barnett for identifying ethnic settlement locations.

Endnotes

1. Richard T. T. Forman, ed., *Pine Barrens: Ecosystem and Landscape* (New York: Academic Press, 1979), xli, Fig. 4.
2. Until the railroads arrived, the southern Pine Barrens was more desolate than the land above the Mullica; see John W. Barber and Henry Howe, *Historical Collections of New Jersey: Past and Present* (Newark, 1865), 64, "This is the most thinly-settled county in the state." Pine Plains once extended into the southern Pine Barrens, too; see Mark N. Demitroff, *Pine Barrens Wetlands: Geographical Reflections of South Jersey's Periglacial Legacy*, MS thesis (Newark, DE: University of Delaware, 2007), 131–32, 149.
3. The Late-Miocene Bridgeton Formation is incised into the Middle Miocene Cohansey. Being less weathered, more clay and nutrients remain. See John C. F. Tedrow, "Development of Pine Barrens Soils," in *Pine Barrens: Ecosystem and Landscape*, ed. Richard T. T. Forman (New York: Academic Press, 1979), 61–79.
4. Originally published as Elizabeth Marsh, "The Southern Pine Barrens: an Ethnic Archipelago," in *Natural and Cultural Resources of the New Jersey Pine Barrens: Inputs and Research Needs for Planning. Proceedings and Papers of the First Research Conference on the New Jersey Pine Barrens, Atlantic City, N.J., May 22–23, 1978*, ed. John W. Sinton (Pomona, NJ: Stockton State College, 1979), 192–98.
5. For more information on these features, including relict plateau, badlands landscape, periglacial mass wasting, see Wayne L. Newell, David S. Powars, James P. Owens, Scott D. Stanford and Byron D. Stone, *Surficial Geologic Map of Central and Southern New Jersey*, United States Geological Survey, Miscellaneous Investigations Series, Map 1-2540-D (Washington, DC, 2000), (Sheet 2, Fig. 4); Hugh M. French, Mark Demitroff, Steven L. Forman and Wayne L. Newell, "A Chronology of Late-Pleistocene Permafrost Events in Southern New Jersey, Eastern USA," *Permafrost and Periglacial Processes* 18, no. 1 (January/March 2007): 49–59.
6. Tedrow, "Development of Pine Barrens Soils," 61–79; J. F. C. Tedrow, *Soils of New Jersey* (Malabar, FL: Robert E. Krieger, 1986), 417–31.
7. Berger and Sinton, *Water, Earth, and Fire*, 84–106; Mark Demitroff, "Sugar Sand Opportunity: Landscape and People of the Pine Barrens," Feature Article, *Vernacular Architecture Newsletter*, summer 2014. http://vafnewsletter.blogspot.com/2014/07/sugar-sand-opportunity-landscape-and.html. Reproduced in the *Vernacular Architecture Newsletter* courtesy of NJ VAF 2014.
8. George H. Cook and Cornelius Clarkson Vermeule, *Atlas of New Jersey*, New Jersey Geologic Survey (New York: Julius Bien, 1889), 20 sheets.
9. Klaus K. E. Neuendorf, James P. Mehl Jr., and Julia A. Jackson, *Glossary of Geology*, 5th ed. (Alexandria, VA: American Geological Institute, 2005), 34: *Archipelago*, "A sea or area in a sea that contains numerous islands; also the island group itself."
10. USDA, "Natural Resources Conservation Service, Hydric Soils —Introduction": *hydric soil*, "A hydric soil is a soil that formed under conditions of saturation, flooding or ponding long enough during the growing season to develop anaerobic conditions in the upper part"; accessed October 8, 2017, https://www.nrcs.usda.gov/wps/portal/nrcs/detail/soils/use/hydric/?cid=nrcs142p2_053961.

11. Ralph W. Tiner Jr., *Wetlands of New Jersey* (Newton Comer, MA: U.S. Fish and Wildlife Service, National Wetlands Inventory, 1985), 42.
12. Jack A. Cresson, Alan Mounier, Anthony Bonfiglio and Mark Demitroff, "Periglacial Landforms of Southern New Jersey: Sites, Trails and Ancient Cultural Links," in *Program and Abstracts, 63rd Eastern Snow Conference, University of Delaware, Held Jointly with the Cryosphere Specialty Group of the Association of American Geographers, 7–9 June 2006*, eds. Robert Hellström and Susan Frankenstein (2006). Demitroff, *Pine Barrens Wetlands*.
13. Neuendorf, *Glossary of Geology*, 331: *interfluve*, "The area between rivers (interstream), esp. the relatively undissected upland or ridge between two adjacent valleys containing streams flowing in the same general direction." Technically, if the interstream terrain is flat and plain-like, the landform may better be described as "doab." See Neuendorf, *Glossary of Geology*, 188: *doab*, "a term applied in the Indo-Gangetic Plain of northern India to the tongue of low-lying alluvial land between two confluent streams . . . commonly restricted to the alluvial plains portion characterized by very low relief."
14. The Pleistocene epoch is the most recent cycles of global ice sheet advances and retreats between 2.58 million and 11.7 thousand years ago, the Ice Age. Philip. L. Gibbard, Martin J. Head, Michael J. C. Walker, and the Subcommission on Quaternary Stratigraphy, "Formal Ratification of the Quaternary System/Period and the Pleistocene Series/Epoch with a Base of 2.58 Ma," *Journal of Quaternary Science* 25, no. 2 (2010): 96–102.
15. South Jersey was formed by the proto-Hudson, a great river estimated to be as much as ten times the size of its modern namesake. In the Middle Miocene, at a time when sea levels were higher than today, the Cohansey Sands and the associated Beacon Hill Gravels were deposited. Later, during the Late Miocene, the ancient proto-Hudson River passed through the lowlands between New Brunswick and Trenton, then followed today's Delaware channel before turning back towards the Atlantic Ocean. Land south of the Mullica was carved into a broad valley, incising (cutting into) the older Cohansey Formation. The younger, less-weathered Bridgeton Formation was deposited. See James P. Owens and James P. Minard, *Upper Cenozoic Sediments of the Lower Delaware Valley and the Northern Delmarva Peninsula, New Jersey, Pennsylvania, Delaware and Maryland*. U.S. Geological Survey Professional Paper 1067-D (Reston, VA, 1979); Newell, *Surficial Geologic Map of Central and Southern New Jersey*.
16. These heights are established by Alexandra Petriman, "Highest Elevations by County in New Jersey, New Jersey Geological and Water Survey Open-File Report 17-1," *New Jersey Geological and Water Survey* (Trenton, NJ, 2017); North American Vertical Datum of 1988 (*NAVD88 Elevation*); Petriman, "Highest Elevations," 8.
17. Petriman, "Highest Elevations," 36.
18. NAVD88.
19. Demitroff, *Pine Barrens Wetlands*; Hugh M. French and Mark Demitroff, "Late-Pleistocene Paleohydrology, Eolian Activity and Frozen Ground, New Jersey Pine Barrens, Eastern USA" *Netherlands Journal of Geosciences* 91, no. 1/2 (2012): 25–35.
20. Modified from Newell et al., *Surficial Geologic Map of Central and Southern New Jersey*, and French et al., "A Chronology of Late-Pleistocene Permafrost Events in Southern New Jersey.
21. Hugh M. French and Mark Demitroff, "Cold-Climate Origin of the Enclosed Depressions and Wetlands ('Spungs') of the Pine Barrens, Southern New Jersey, USA," *Permafrost and Periglacial Processes* 12, no. 4 (December 2001): 337–50; Demitroff, *Pine Barrens Wetlands*, 45–78.
22. Demitroff, *Pine Barrens Wetlands*, 79–99.
23. Hugh M. French, Mark Demitroff and Steve L. Forman, "Evidence for Late-Pleistocene Thermokarst in the New Jersey Pine Barrens (Latitude 39 Degree N), Eastern USA," Permafrost and Periglacial Processes 16, no. 2 (2005): 173–86.
24. Demitroff, "Sugar Sand Opportunity."
25. Marsh used the term "Sequent Occupance," an archaic concept in geography, now refined as human geography. Kent Mathewson, "Sequent Occupance," *The International Encyclopedia of Geography* (John Wiley & Sons, Ltd., 2016), accessed November 27, 2017, http://onlinelibrary.wiley.com/doi/10.1002/9781118786352.wbieg0015/full; Demitroff, "Sugar Sand Opportunity."
26. Another valued landform eluded Marsh's original work, being the higher ground closest to the southeast rims of ponds located in the wetlands at stream headlands. These closed basins, colloquially known as spungs, were important places of transhumance for 14,000 years. Two examples, out of many, are Hospitality Ponds at Squankum and Lochs-of-the-Swamp at Indiantown. See Anthony Bonfiglio and John A. Cresson, "Geomorphology and Pinelands Prehistory: a Model into Early Aboriginal Land Use," in *History, Culture and Archeology of the New Jersey Pine Barrens*, ed. John. W. Sinton (Pomona, NJ: Center for Environmental Research, Stockton State College, 1982), 15–67; Jack A. Cresson, et al., "Periglacial Landforms of Southern New Jersey," 72; Demitroff, *Pine Barrens Wetlands*.
27. Overlooked in Marsh's original thesis were the cedar industry and naval stores. See Peter Kalm's 1770 account on cedar in *Peter Kalm's Travels in North America—The America of 1750*, 2 vol., revised and adapted from the original Swedish and edited by Adolph B. Benson (New York: Dover Publications, 1964), 20; Harry B. Weiss and Grace M. Weiss, *Trades and Tradesmen of Colonial New Jersey* (Trenton: Past Times Press, 1965), 70; Demitroff, "Sugar Sand Opportunity."
28. Demitroff, *Pine Barrens Wetlands*, 124–150.
29. Arthur D. Pierce, *Iron in the Pines: The Story of New Jersey's Ghost Towns and Bog Iron* (New Brunswick, NJ: Rutgers University Press, 1957); Arthur D. Pierce, *Family Empire in Jersey Iron: the Richards Enterprises in the Pine Barrens* (New Brunswick, NJ: Rutgers University Press, 1964).

30 W. George Cook and William J. Coxey, *Atlantic City Railroad: Royal Route to the* Sea (Oaklyn, NJ: West Jersey Chapter, National Railway Historical Society, Inc., 1980); Richard J. Gladulich, *By Rail to the Boardwalk* (Trans-Anglo Books, 1986); Christopher T. Baer, William J. Coxey, and Paul W. Schopp, *Trail of the Blue Comet: A History of the New Jersey Central's Southern Division* (Palmyra, NJ: West Jersey Chapter, National Railway Historical Society, Inc., 1994).

31 Customarily "marl," as applied in New Jersey, is a pseudomarl composed of mica pellets surrounded by a plaster-of-Paris-like coating of glauconite. See John C. F. Tedrow, *Greensand and Greensand Soils of New Jersey: A Review*, E279, Department of Ecology, Evolution and Natural Resources, Rutgers University, New Brunswick, NJ, 2002; cf. true marl of the Vincentown Formation, see Henri Bader and Peter E. Wolfe, *The Lime Marl Deposit of Vincentown, New Jersey*, Bulletin No. 3, Bureau of Mineral Research, Rutgers University, New Brunswick, NJ, 1948.

32 Forman, 1979, 17.

33 John R. Mather, Marie Sanderson, *The Genius of C. Warren Thornthwaite, Climatologist-Geographer* (Norman and London: University of Oklahoma Press, 1996).

34 Edmund Morris, *Ten Acres Enough: A Practical Experience, Showing How a Very Small Farm May be Made to Keep a Very Large Family with Extensive and Profitable Experience in the Cultivation of the Smaller Fruits* (New York: James Miller, 1864).

35 William Paul Dillingham, *Immigrants in Industries (in Twenty-Five Parts), Part 24: Recent Immigrants in Agriculture* (in 2 vols, vol. 1), Document No. 633, Reports of the Immigration Commission, Washington, DC, 1911; Demitroff, "Sugar Sand Opportunity."

36 Gertrude M. Eckhardt, *The History of Folsom, New Jersey: 1845–1976. Bicentennial Edition* (Egg Harbor City, NJ: Laureate Press, 1973); Dieter Cunz, "Egg Harbor City: New Germany in New Jersey," *Report of the Society of the Germans in Maryland* 29 (1956): 9–30.

37 A. G. Warner, "Sketches, Incidents and History of Vineland," *Vineland and the Vinelanders* (Vineland, NJ: F. P. Crocker, 1869), reprinted in *The Vineland Historical Magazine* Vol. 57, no. 1, 1981, 18–71; Benjamin F. Ladd and Wanser and Osgood, *History of Vineland* (Vineland, NJ: Evening Journal Book and Job Printing Establishment, 1881), reprinted in *The Vineland Historical Magazine* Vol. 51, nos. 1&2, 1974, 1–64; H. W. Wilbur and W. B. Hand, *Illustrated History of the Town of Hammonton: With an Account of its Soil, Climate and Industries* (Hammonton, NJ: The Mirror Steam Printing Co, 1889); reprint, Hammonton Historical Society, 1977); William McMahon, *The Story of Hammonton: A History of the Town of Hammonton* (Egg Harbor City, NJ: Laureate Press, 1966).

38 Emily Fogg Meade, "The Italian on the Land: A Study in Immigration," *Bulletin of the Bureau of Labor* 70 (1907): reprinted by the Hammonton Historical Society, 1992, 1–78; Dillingham, *Reports of the Immigration Commission*, 38–137.

39 Joseph Brandes, *Immigrants to Freedom: Jewish Communities in Rural New Jersey Since 1882* (Philadelphia: The Jewish Publication Society of America, 1971); Allen Meyers, *Southern New Jersey Synagogues: A Social History Highlighted by Stories of Jewish Life from the 1880's–1980's* (Sewell, NJ: Sir Speedy Printers, 1990); Ellen Eisenberg, *Jewish Agricultural Colonies in New Jersey, 1882–1920* (Syracuse, NY: Syracuse University Press, 1995).

40 Michael Aaron Rockland, "Meet the Kalmyks," *New Jersey Monthly*, March 14, 2011, accessed December 6, 2017, https://njmonthly.com/articles/jersey-living/meet-the-kalmyks/; David Wallenchinsky and Irving Wallace, *The People's Almanac #2: A Completely New Book from Cover to Cover* (New York: William Morrow, 1978), 655; J. McElhatton, "Fading Icon of Hope," *Press of Atlantic City,* D1, August 11, 2002; Wallace McKelvey, "Preserving Cossack history in Buena Vista Township" *Press of Atlantic City*, April 2, 2013, accessed December 6, 2017, http://www.pressofatlanticcity.com/news/press/new_jersey/preserving-cossack-history-in-buena-vista-township/article_128df5aa-aae0-11e2-9c2b-0019bb2963f4.html; Dennis Mikolay, *Here, in This Forgotten Place.*, manuscript in progress.

41 Kathryn H. Chalmers, *Down the Long-a-Coming* (Moorestown, NJ: The News Chronicle, 1951); G. M. Eckhardt, *The History of Folsom, New Jersey: 1845–1976. Bicentennial Edition* (Egg Harbor City, NJ: Laureate Press, 1975).

42 Nativity of emigres to Mullica and Galloway Township and Egg Harbor City for 1850, 1860, and 1870: In 1850, Mullica Township had a population of 32 immigrants from Germany; Galloway Township, 6; and Egg Harbor City (yet to be populated), 0. In 1860, Mullica Township had a population of 89 immigrants from Germany; Galloway Township, 644; Egg Harbor City, 691. In 1870, Mullica Township had a population of 41 from Germany, Prussia, and other German states; Galloway Township, 193; and Egg Harbor City, 614. Source: Federal decennial censuses for years and municipalities detailed.

43 Germans had developed agricultural techniques to farm poor soils of their Great Sand Belt, which covers most of Prussia, a half-century earlier, Demitroff, "Sugar Sand Opportunity."

44 Frederick W. Beers, *Topographic Map of Atlantic County, New Jersey, from Recent and Actual Surveys* (New York: Beers, Comstock & Cline, 1872); *A Farm within the Reach of Every Man: Weymouth Land and Agricultural Company*, sales prospectus (n.p., 1854).

45 The Germans fail to show up to pick crops in 1877, and Southern Italians and Sicilians replace them. Landis already had a corner on Northern Italian labor. Dillingham, *Reports of the Immigration Commission*, 100.

46 "City Affairs—The Weymouth Land Association—an Alleged Conspiracy to Defraud," *North American and United States Gazette*, August 10, 1858, 1.

47 In 1870, Hammonton contained 1404 inhabitants versus Vineland's 7040 residents per the federal decennial census

48 Robert F. Johnson, *Weymouth New Jersey: A History of the Furnace, Forge, and Paper Mills* (Kearney, NE: Morris Publishing, 2001).
49 *Vineland Historical Magazine,* Vol. 1, no. 1, 1916, 2.
50 Demitroff, "Sugar Sand Opportunity."
51 The 1870 federal census recorded 7,040 residents within the bounds of Vineland.
52 "Gloucester Farm and Town Association," *Daily Pennsylvanian*, November 18, 1854, 2.
53 "A German City . . .," *Newark Daily Advertiser*, December 3, 1856, 2.
54 Eugene V. Young and Elaine Conover Abrahamson, *The Story of Galloway Township* (Egg Harbor City, NJ: The Laureate Press for The Galloway Township Bicentennial Committee, 1976), 25–29.
55 Demitroff, "Sugar Sand Opportunity."
56 Demitroff, "Sugar Sand Opportunity."
57 "Pennsylvania-Reading Seashore Lines, West Jersey & Seashore R.R. Co," Coverdale and Colpitts, *The Pennsylvania Railroad Company: The Corporate, Financial and Construction History of Lines Owned, Operated and Controlled to December 31, 1945, Volume IV, Affiliated Lines, Miscellaneous Companies, and General Index* ([Philadelphia]: Pennsylvania Railroad, [1949]), 168.
58 Meyers, *Southern New Jersey Synagogues*, 1990.
59 Marsh gained much inspiration from the classical work of Carl Ortwin Sauer, an early cultural geographer who reconstructed past cultural landscapes where culture (humans) are the agents of change. Sauer asserted that their given landscape becomes the medium of modification, which results in the formation of a distinct cultural landscape (e.g., Carl O. Sauer, "The Morphology of Landscape," *University of California Publications in Geography* 2 [1925]). Nature does not make culture (environmental determinism); culture instead accommodates nature through adaptation and this is how a population actually arrives at a distinct way of life. An ethnic archipelago is a human manifestation, not a product of physical conditions present in the Pine Barrens. Sauer was schooled in Germany, returning to study geology, then switched to geography. Sequential Occupation in geography is a chronological approach to regional identity, as Derwent Whittlesey proposed in, "Sequent Occupance," *Annals of the Association of American Geographers* 19 (1929): 162–66. There is a generational succession of landscape modifications that gives us a distinctive cultural landscape at any given moment. A case might be made that this spirited argument against environmental determinism in the Pine Barrens changed the world. Hammonton's Margaret Mead, an anthropologist of great renown—along with her mother Emily Fogg Meade, studied the area's social landscape (see Patricia Chappine and Mark Demitroff, "Where Blackberries Grew: Margaret Mead in Hammonton," *SoJourn* Vol. 1, no. 2 (Winter 2016/17), 37–43. Margaret was mentored by German-American anthropologist Franz Boas. It was Boas, not Sauer, who railed against the concept of the now marginalized environmental determinism, a concept that buoyed social Darwinism and smacked of racism and rationalized economic inequality.
60 Dillingham, *Reports of the Immigration Commission*, 100.
61 Gabriel Donio, *Images of America: Hammonton* (Charleston, SC: Arcadia Publishing, 2002), 8.
62 Mexican and Central Americans. See Cindy Hahamovitch, *The Fruits of Their Labor: Atlantic Coast Farmworkers and the Making of Migrant Poverty, 1870–1945* (Chapel Hill, University of North Carolina Press, 1997).
63 Brandes, *Immigrants to Freedom*; Eisenberg, *Jewish Agricultural Colonies in New Jersey, 1882–1920*.
64 Meyers, *Southern New Jersey Synagogues*.
65 Demitroff, "Sugar Sand Opportunity."
66 Meyers, *Southern New Jersey Synagogues*, 310–312
67 Mikolay, manuscript in progress,
68 The unnamed early twentieth century "community of Finns" in Atlantic County, which Marsh mentioned in her original article, is likely Finn Town at Sweetwater's High Bank along the Mullica River—with cabins and saunas (Personal communications, Carl Farrell, December 3, 2017; and Robert Barnett, February 24, 2018).
69 Ron Avery, "Black Jews Find Home in Jersey Pines," *Philadelphia Daily News*, June 10, 1985, 10.
70 The spelling of the planned settlement of Montefiore is a matter of some dispute. The name, presumably, was meant to associate the real-estate venture with the nineteenth-century philanthropist Moses Montefiore. The town plans shown on pages 16–17 spell the name as Montefiore. Several other documents, however, spell the name "Montefiroe," perhaps for legal reasons since the planned town, in fact, was not supported by the philanthropist. David M. Razler references the name Montefiroe from Gershenowitz's review of tax maps in "Mystery, Scandal Mask Towns's Demise," *Press of Atlantic City* (April 3, 1988), A1. Map No. 1 of Cape May Land & Building Company at Halberton (1891) references Montefiroe. Charles S. Hartman compiled maps from searches made at the courthouses of Bridgeton, Salem, Cape May, Mays Landing, Woodbury, and Gloucester, and from ancient survey maps made by old surveyors; his maps one and three (of eight) reference Montefiro. Finally, Virgil S. Johnson, author of *Millville Glass: The Early Days* (1971), in an undated ms. for his "Ramblin' Round—Memory Lane" for the *Millville Daily*, uses Montefiroe; a xerographic copy of this manuscript can be found in the Millville Historical Society collection.
71 Meyers 1990, 76–79; Wendel A. White, *Small Towns, Black Lives* (Oceanville, NJ: The Noyes Museum of Art, 2003), 153–61.
72 Mikolay, in press; Wallenchinsky and Wallace, 1978, 655.
73 Collin Black, "Gypsy Patriarch: 'We're Not Going to Live Like Pigs,' *Asbury Park Press*, Sunday, April 15, 1979, A20.
74 The co-authors are unable to pinpoint the bounds of this small Polish settlement in Absecon Highlands, but 6.5 percent of those residing within the community reportedly

have Polish ancestry (see https://www.neighborhoodscout.com/nj/absecon/demographics).

75 Originally published as Elizabeth Marsh, "The Southern Pine Barrens: an Ethnic Archipelago," in *Natural and Cultural Resources of the New Jersey Pine Barrens: Inputs and Research Needs for Planning. Proceedings and Papers of the First Research Conference on the New Jersey Pine Barrens, Atlantic City, N.J., May 22–23, 1978*, ed. John W. Sinton (Pomona, NJ: Stockton State College, 1979), 192–98. see also Jonathan Berger and John W. Sinton, *Water, Earth, and Fire: Land Use and Environmental Planning in the New Jersey Pine Barrens* (Baltimore, MD: The Johns Hopkins University Press, 1985), 84–106. Libby also published "An Introduction to South Jersey," *Echoes of History* 5, no. 3 (August 1975): 1, 38–39; and *Cooperative Rural Planning: A Tug Hill Case Study*, (Watertown, N.Y: Temporary State Commission on Tug Hill, 1981).

76 "Alfred C. Redfield," *Biographical Memoirs*, vol. 67 (The National Academics of Sciences, Academics, and Medicine, 1995), https://www.nap.edu/read/4894/chapter/16#315; "In Memoriam, Elizabeth Redfield Marsh '45," *Reed Magazine* (September 2011), http://www.reed.edu/reed-magazine/in-memoriam/obituaries/september2011/elizabeth-redfield-marsh-1945.html.

77 "Lighthouse Shines for Tourists," *Register Star* (Rockford, Illinois), December 9, 1979; "Jersey's Lighthouses are Beacons of Lore for the History Buff," *Newark Star-Ledger* (October 28, 1984), 1, 5.

Although the location of this picker's shack is uncertain, H. Kelly, the young man standing on the roof, penned a message and mailed the card from Cologne, New Jersey, to the Home Missionary Society on Arch Street in Philadelphia on July 21, 1908. Master Kelly wrote: "Dear Sir, I will sent you a card of our S. Berries field & Picker house. I am on top of the house. I made a cross [actually ink dots] which is our family. We picked 500 crates of Straw Berries. . . . I did not pick many; I helped in side. Please let me [know] if got the card." The Home Missionary Society was an outreach agency of the Presbyterian Church to provide agricultural workers with social services and simple medical care.

A bullfrog in Muddy Bog, a favorite wetland at Unexpected Wildlife Refuge.

Miller Pond, one of the major wetlands at Unexpected Wildlife Refuge.

Unexpected Wildlife Refuge:
Haven for South Jersey Wildlife

Nedim C. Buyukmihci

The co-founders of the Refuge were my parents, Hope Sawyer Buyukmihci and Cavit Buyukmihci. Hope was an impassioned naturalist, artist, activist and writer. Her compassion was infectious and Cavit, a metallurgical engineer, soon fully embraced an ethic of reverence for all life.

One of my most vivid childhood memories is finding a snake in the woods surrounding our home in South Jersey, to which we had just moved by way of Turkey. I desperately wanted to catch and closely observe this individual, but my father was concerned for my "safety." My mother, however, knew that most snakes were harmless to people and overruled my father. Thus began our family's journey into wildlife, involving much education, revelation and self-sacrifice. We became known as the people who were "animal nuts" and who vigorously opposed hunting and trapping.

For years, my mother yearned to spend more time observing and drawing wildlife. She and my father began a search for a small plot of natural or near-natural land which my mother could use as her studio. In 1961, they purchased an 85-acre tract in Buena Vista Township, located in the Pinelands. Mostly wooded swampland, the property included a rustic cabin, an old barn, and a stream which beavers had dammed to create a large pond where once a cranberry bog had existed. It was an ideal place for my mother to get intimately involved with wildlife. We soon decided that it was also a wonderful place to live, made modest improvements to the cabin, and moved there permanently.

Spicebush swallowtail butterfly near a trail.

Hope and Cavit recognized early on that the biggest threat to wildlife involves loss of habitat through destruction or fragmentation. As a result, they donated their land and home to begin Unexpected Wildlife Refuge, named after Unexpected Road, off which it is situated. The Refuge became incorporated as a non-profit organization in 1968 and received federal tax-exempt status in 1969.

Since then, the Refuge has added other parcels of contiguous land so that today it encompasses 767 acres of vital habitat comprising fields, wetlands, forests, bogs, and standing ponds. This provides living opportunities for hundreds of species of amphibians, birds, insects, mammals, reptiles and other animals, and plants. Some are considered biologically threatened (Pine Barrens tree frog), endangered (red-bellied turtle), or scarce (southern twayblade orchid and wild lupine, the latter which is the only known host plant for the nationally endangered butterfly, the Karner blue).

From its inception, the Refuge has remained undeveloped and wild. It is one of the few places where wildlife are considered the primary benefactors with human interests a distant second. Everything we do is geared toward minimal intervention so that animals (and plants) can exist consistent with their needs and desires. There is no manipulation of habitat to encourage one species over another, no artificial feeding or housing. Wildlife are essentially in complete control of their destiny. Trails for human access are kept to a minimum in number and scope, and primarily so that this relatively vast area can be patrolled to keep out people intent on destroying wildlife. The trails also serve to allow visitors to tour and view this diverse habitat with a minimum of disturbance to the inhabitants. No boating or other access into any of the ponds or lakes is permitted. Hunting, fishing, trapping, and other consumptive exploitation have always been prohibited. Peaceful coexistence with wildlife is a key part of wildlife and habitat protection and the Refuge extends its influence beyond its borders to help the public achieve this principle elsewhere.

In order to help wildlife here and outside our borders, we provide educational tours of the Refuge, as well as presentations to schools and others groups, always striving to help resolve human-wildlife conflicts peacefully and without detriment to the wildlife. In particular, we work with individuals and municipalities within the state and beyond to educate people on ways to live in harmony with wildlife who may be perceived as causing problems. Our most successful efforts have been in protecting resident beaver families from extirpation when people were concerned about trees and flooding.

Managing a wildlife refuge on land formerly used by local people and others for fishing, hunting, and trapping for decades was not easy. We struggled for many years to "teach" those people that this type of exploitation was no longer allowed. For a while, trespassing to fish, hunt, and trap occurred regularly. I vividly remember encounters with hunters during which heated words were exchanged and, in at least two situations, our lives were threatened verbally and by the discharge of a firearm. I am grateful that those early days of strife appear to have diminished and, today, trespassing to destroy wildlife is kept in check by peaceful patrolling and education.

We also became educated by our interaction with others. When we asked one hunter why he chose to hunt and kill animals, he replied by asking if we ate cows or chickens. When we answered truthfully that we did, the hunter said that the deer and quail he killed were

Aerial view of main pond and surrounds. Photograph courtesy Cliff Compton.

Delicate dragonfly poised near the edge of the main pond.

Common bog violet.

Black racer near one of the trails.

Wild turkeys who "took" their own photo via trail camera.

his "cows and chickens." This exchange was one of the important experiences that made us realize that personal choices in food and fiber were critical to not only being morally consistent on a personal level, but also in being credible to those who exploited and killed animals for any purpose regardless of species. We asked ourselves the question of why a cow's life was any less important than that of the deer we were protecting and found the answer to be exceedingly simple: life and being able to pursue one's interests were equally important *to the*

Beaver eating a water lily in the main pond.

Family of Canada geese in the main pond.

White-tailed deer spending time on one of several islands in the main pond.

individual regardless of species. We realized that one cannot effectively advocate for the protection of wildlife without also refraining from exploiting animals, not only those who are held in captivity to provide food and fiber for people, but also in all areas of human activity. We discontinued eating animals and soon thereafter embraced veganism as a way of life.

Although the Refuge charter did not address the issue of veganism, we are aware that this is a pivotal issue. We recognize that being a vegan because one is concerned about others who share this planet with us extends beyond just dietary choices. It governs everything we do, all the choices we make each day, in order to minimize our negative impact on all animals. We also are aware that a vegan diet and choice of clothing are superior, not only because of the direct impact on other animals, but also because of the detrimental effects that animal-based food and fiber have on the environment and all who inhabit this earth. In addition to the suffering and death inflicted on the animals raised for human consumption, there are other issues such as air and water pollution, destruction of wildlife to protect livestock, destruction of habitat due to livestock grazing and so forth.

Volunteers have played an important part in keeping the Refuge safe and accessible for educational purposes. Humane-minded individuals have helped us patrol the borders during so-called hunting seasons in order to deter hunters from encroaching on animals in the Refuge. Often freezing temperatures and difficult terrain make their efforts a true labor of love. Young volunteers from groups like the Boy Scouts and YMCA have given their time in maintaining some of the trails and signs. Each year, people spend a day with us on or around Earth Day, clearing trash from various locations that border public land.

Cavit died July 25, 1987, shortly after he had retired with the plan of spending more time protecting the Refuge and becoming more involved in the cause of animal protection. Hope continued to run the Refuge with the help of dedicated volunteers, supported entirely by private donations from visitors. She died June 20, 2001. Although these two stalwart and dedicated people no longer are here, their legacy and message of compassion for all life continue unabated. Stewardship of the Refuge remains in the capable hands of the Council of Trustees,

Juvenile hog-nosed snake assuming a threatening pose to ward off danger;
One of the many swampy areas of forest;
The colorful purple turkey-tail fungus;
A resident river otter, "caught" by a trail camera.

committed to providing a home to all wildlife—animals and plants—native to the region. The Refuge has always been frugal in its management, never having more than one paid employee. The latter is a manager, living on-site and providing a positive presence throughout the year. Extensive use of volunteers has kept operating costs to a minimum. Nevertheless, we are always in need of funds and volunteers and urge people to participate in whatever way they can. Please visit our Web site to learn more about us and for ways to provide support.

(http://unexpectedwilliferefuge.org/)

About the Author

Dr. Buyukmihci received his veterinary medical degree from the University of Pennsylvania and has spent most of his adult life working on animal protection issues. He is currently Emeritus Professor of Veterinary Medicine at the University of California-Davis and resides in the United Kingdom with his wife and rescued chickens and dogs.

Main pond at height of summer. Photograph courtesy of Dave Sauder (a Refuge Trustee).

The Sphinx Woman

Patricia A. Martinelli

The 1920s roared through New Jersey as violently as through the rest of America. In the struggling post-war economy, the Garden State weathered crooked politicians, gangsters brazenly defying the Volstead Act, and scandalous murders like the Lilliendahl case in rural Vineland.[1] But even the most hardened New Jersey residents cringed when confronted by the story of Gladys May Parks.

The newspapers had a lot of names for the pretty 35-year-old brunette defendant in the bizarre murder case that shocked the 1929 public. "Midnight May" was popular for a while,[2] as was "Stone Woman" and "Iron Woman,"[3] but the one that stuck best was the "Sphinx Woman."[4] Throughout her trial for the murder of two siblings—four-year-old Dorothy and two-year-old Timothy Rogers—Parks sat stone-faced at the defendant's table in the Camden courtroom. Those present gasped over the lurid details of the trial as they came to light, but Parks appeared oblivious to what was going on around her, at least until Supreme Court Judge Frank T. Lloyd handed down her sentence. When she learned that she was going to serve twenty-five years of hard labor in the Clinton Reformatory for Women for the murder of the Rogers children, Parks finally fell apart.

Did Parks feel remorse, realizing the magnitude of what she had done? No, more likely Parks was only sorry she had gotten caught.

After all, getting involved with the Rogers children had not been part of the plan. Born on May 17, 1894, in the tiny riverfront town of Mays Landing, Gladys May Parks once had big dreams of becoming a star. She supported herself since the age of fifteen, playing piano in movie houses and casinos. There were times when she had to work as a sales clerk in a department store to pay the rent, but the real plan had been to make it as an entertainer.[5]

In the years prior to her conviction for murder, Parks had moved from city to city up and down the east coast, always in search of her big break. It was possible that she had stayed on the move because she feared being arrested for the occasional petty crime, like shoplifting or skimming cash from her register at work. It was also possible she inherited the traveling gene from her father, Benjamin Parks, an itinerant glassblower who

Gladys May Parks, the Sphinx Woman, whose sensational story was told in the pages of newspapers across the country. This image was often reproduced.

constantly relocated his family wherever work could be found.[6]

When the years had passed and the dream of stardom seemed no closer, Parks was finally lured back to South Jersey by the bright lights of Atlantic City. There she met Anthony Baker at a dance on the Million Dollar Pier. She would later refer to herself as "Mrs. Baker" on occasion, and often flaunted both a diamond engagement ring and a diamond-studded wedding band, but there was never any evidence that the couple had married.[7] She continued to work as a sales clerk by day and sought singing jobs at night in the casinos and honky-tonks that clustered near the boardwalk. Life might be tough for most Americans, but they knew how to have a good time in Atlantic City.

Early in 1929, with stardom still eluding her, Parks moved with Baker to Brooklawn, a small community in Camden County, just over the bridge from Philadelphia. Shortly thereafter, during one of their many separations, Parks—who was then living in Camden—learned that her cousin Olive had died suddenly, leaving behind a husband and six children.

Mild-mannered Woodbury insurance salesman Allen Rogers was emotionally devastated after the death of his wife. He was not prepared to say "no" when Parks approached him with a generous proposition in April of that year. She offered to take the two youngest of his six children, Dorothy and Timothy, to live with her and her husband to relieve Rogers of the burden of supporting such a large family.[8] She assured the bewildered widower that she and her husband had the finances to ensure that the children would live comfortably, receive a good education, and enjoy the opportunity to travel.

With practiced ease, Parks reminded Rogers that he also had little chance of remarrying with such a large brood.[9] Although he was reluctant at first, Rogers finally relented, allowing her to take away his two youngest on May 31, 1929. That was the last time he would see them alive.

Contrary to the web of lies that she had spun for the distraught father, Parks was accompanied by her 64-year-old father when she set up housekeeping with the children on June 2 in a Camden rooming house. In the weeks that followed, Rogers made a number of attempts to speak to his children, but Parks always had an excuse as to why they were not available. It was not until too late that he discovered the wealthy "husband" she claimed was not in the picture.

Always afraid that Rogers would see through her stories and come and take the children away, Parks moved out and rented new rooms in Camden under a different name. Rogers finally tracked her to the first apartment a few weeks later. Parks and the children had disappeared. Neither her father, who had been left behind, nor the neighbors, knew where they had gone. The neighbors regaled him with horror stories about the ways that the children were being badly mistreated by the woman who had assured him she would give them a good home. One neighbor later told the press that Parks had often made "mysterious jaunts" after midnight, leaving the two youngsters alone in the apartment all night long.

Increasingly desperate, Rogers kept searching, spurred on by a letter that Parks sent him that August.[10] She accused him of spreading lies about her, adding: "If you had been more considerate and not such a glutton for children, Olive would have been alive today."

Rogers finally went to the police to report that his children were missing—a story that was quickly picked up by newspapers across the United States. The investigation into their disappearance made little progress until the morning of November 2, when a group of girls walking to church in National Park, Gloucester County, made a gruesome discovery. Some bones from a child's skeleton buried in a shallow grave had been scattered by wild animals. Some of the remains lay partially wrapped in a sheet with a Camden laundry mark.

At that time, Parks had been hiding out with her on-again, off-again "husband," Anthony Baker, at 101 Warren Street in Newark.[11] When she read of the discovery and that the police wanted her for questioning about the children, Parks walked into the local police headquarters and turned herself in, informing the police that she was an unmarried waitress. Baker, who was then working at an automobile factory, told authorities that he knew nothing of the fate of the children—a fact that Parks corroborated. All the same, he was brought to Camden with her and held as a material witness.[12]

Once the remains from National Park were identified as those of Dorothy Rogers, the police began questioning Parks in earnest. She held fast to the claim that she had accidentally killed Dorothy by slapping her too hard. When asked about Timothy, she said he had died in an accidental fall on the stairs. Despite her insistence that she was not really at fault in either instance, authorities soon learned that there was a darker motive behind her offer to care for the Rogers children.

It was not out of loyalty to her cousin or any maternal instinct. Instead, she had apparently used the children in a ploy to blackmail prominent, unsuspecting men, three from Atlantic City and four from Philadelphia.[13] Parks would select her target and present the children as his, promising to disappear from his life for a small fee. Before too long, however, she discovered that her biggest problem was not the authorities or Allan Rogers—it was the children themselves.

Dorothy proved to be difficult, her behavior not surprising, given the circumstances. Taken from her home and her family after losing her mother at such a young age, she was unable to adjust to a new life with this strange woman who never seemed to have a kind word for her or Timothy. So she acted out, as any child would do. Parks later told the police that the child was "difficult" and had a "bad habit" that she repeatedly tried to correct, although she never specifically explained the problem.[14] Dorothy's behavior annoyed her so much that on August 7, she beat the little girl to death. Seventeen days later, Timothy was also dead.

When questioned by authorities about the little boy's death, Parks claimed that she had been sorting laundry when she heard a scream and rushed out to find him lying at the foot of the stairs. She allegedly carried him into the kitchen to wash the blood from his face but, within minutes, he was dead in her arms.[15] However, the autopsy revealed that Timothy had been killed by a heavy blow to his head, his skull fractured in two places.

Transferred to Camden County Jail following her arrest on November 11, the police subjected her almost immediately to twenty-five hours of intensive interrogation regarding the fate of the Rogers children. She was transported to the apartment house where the children had died, barely escaping being lynched by a crowd of angry neighbors.[16] Unfazed by their taunts, Parks calmly reiterated her story once again.

She told police that she had panicked after Dorothy died. In reality, she was clear-headed enough to hide the child's body in a suitcase, which she then stashed for a time in the closet of yet a different apartment. Later, she covered the body with lye and buried it in the cellar of the apartment house where she resided. His sister's body was still in the cellar when Timothy died.[17]

Parks told authorities that she later dug a shallow grave near National Park in which she buried the little girl. Once she had removed Dorothy's remains from the apartment house, Parks went to a store in Camden to purchase a black bag in which she placed Timothy's body. Catching a bus for Absecon, she got off near the State Police headquarters, walked several blocks to a cemetery and buried his remains there in the underbrush. When she missed the last bus back to Camden, she tried to contact a friend in Atlantic City, but found herself spending the night alone in a hotel.[18]

Despite the gaps in her story, Parks refused to provide further details. Camden County Prosecutor Clifford Baldwin and a team of detectives worked in relays around the clock to fill in those gaps, but no matter how hard they pushed, Parks maintained a stoic silence regarding to any further particulars.[19]

In the week that followed, she continued to be questioned at irregular intervals. Although she was allowed periodic breaks to eat, the police would not let her sleep. Baldwin was determined to "break her down." By that point, the papers described Parks as haggard and red-eyed, but she never admitted any more of the story.[20]

Yet if the deaths were accidental, then why did she not contact the police or the children's father? Why did she later bury the bodies of the children in obscure locations? No matter how hard the police pressed her, according to the newspapers, Parks insisted: "I am telling you the truth. Honestly, I am."[21]

Baldwin was determined to secure a confession from the woman in order to pursue murder charges in court, but she refused to break under questioning. Baldwin is reported to have said:

> We just can't do a thing with her.... She called every witness a liar when his statement differed from hers. She has called me a liar so often I am beginning to doubt my own veracity. Everybody is lying, the way she puts it.[22]

Baldwin believed that

> She has built up a clever tissue of lies designed to shield herself.... She has confessed to nothing that is more damaging than involuntary manslaughter, but I believe she lies.[23]

Unfortunately, Parks refused to say anything that would qualify as an outright confession, even after witnesses contradicted her story. The police even brought in some of her former lovers and were shocked when they learned that Parks had apparently used as many as four other children in her blackmail schemes.[24] Detective Sergeant Louis Shaw learned about the other children when none of the men they contacted recognized Dorothy or Timothy. The newspapers noted that Shaw said, "We have been unable to discover what has become of those children and we suspect that she may have done with them what she did with Dorothy and Timmie."[25] Detectives pronounced Parks the "coolest, most cold-blooded creature they ever had anything to do with."[26]

And still, Parks remained silent. The prosecutor realized he was going to have to proceed to court without her confession.

Although Parks remained calm during most of her arraignment before Judge Garfield Pancoast, she gasped when the clerk read the murder charges. When the judge asked her how she wanted to plead, Parks responded, "Well, I didn't intend to kill her."[27] She opted to plead not guilty because she felt she had not, in fact, committed murder.

On January 13, 1930, Parks was brought to trial in Camden before Supreme Court Judge Frank T. Lloyd and charged with two counts of murder in the first degree.[28]

The public was banned from the trial because authorities feared there would be violence. Newspapers across America avidly followed the story, provided by Associated Press reporters who haunted the courtroom each day. No detail was too small for public consumption. According to an account in the *Reading Times*:

> Arising early, Gladys Parks faced the day of her trial with prayer on her knees, in her cell. Then after breakfasting, she spent the ensuing hours primping for her first appearance in court. She groomed herself carefully, brushing her hair three times before she was summoned to court. Her principal concern appeared to be the selection of a dress from her fairly complete wardrobe, and she tried one after the other before reaching a satisfactory selection.[29]

Occasionally, Parks appeared discomfited by some of the evidence—especially when the prosecutor talked about the discovery of the skeletons. But the quivering chin and moist eyes may have been an act for the twelve members of the all-male jury, rather than due to any real emotion.

Defended by court-appointed attorneys Samuel Orlando and Carl Kisselman, she most often stared steadily ahead as she sat at the defendant's table, occasionally even falling asleep.[30] At other times, Parks paid more attention to the sketches of the newspaper artists than she did to the progress of the trial.

When she was examined during the trial, Parks offered no less than six different theories on what had happened to the children. They ranged from total innocence in any involvement in their deaths to trying to blame Timothy's death on Joseph Corio of Atlantic City, a judge associated with political boss Enoch ("Nucky") Johnson and facing charges of income tax evasion. Parks even noted that her brother-in-law, Earl Farr, had been an accessory to the murder. According to the defendant, Corio had flown into a rage when she claimed that Timothy was his son.[31]

She then described in graphic detail how he murdered the child. But a few days later, after detectives investigated her claims, Parks recanted the story.[32] She said the prosecutor had confused her through constantly questioning her without a break for rest. She added that she accused Corio, a wealthy and influential man, because he was in a better position than she to avoid serving time in jail.

When Corio took the stand, he claimed that he had not seen Parks since 1926, when she asked him to handle a small estate claim for her family. He was able to prove that he had been in Atlantic City on August 2, the day Parks asserted that he had murdered Timothy. Other witnesses called to the stand corroborated Corio's testimony.[33]

During the trial, her attorneys hinted that Parks was probably insane; she had a history of a violent temper caused by contracting influenza as a child. Although a few witnesses came forward to testify on her behalf, on January 18, 1930, the jury found her guilty of manslaughter and second-degree murder of Dorothy and Timothy respectively.

Two days later, she was sentenced and the first cracks in her calm facade appeared. Returned to her cell to await transport, Parks reportedly flew into a rage and cried, "I won't be in any prison long . . . They'll take me out in a wooden box."[34]

Interestingly enough, Parks was not destined to be bound by the judge's ruling for very long. After serving roughly seven months of her sentence at the Clinton reformatory, she began to show signs of mental instability, forcing authorities to call in a psychiatrist. Shortly thereafter, Commissioner William J. Ellis released a brief statement indicating that Parks would be committed to the Trenton State Hospital for the Insane on August 29, 1930, based on the doctors' assessment.[35] Newspaper reports noted that, "The woman's mind has been failing for the past three months. Haunted by the memory of the children, she has gradually drifted from one hallucination to another, until she became subject to violent fits."[36] She was 36 years old at the time.

Little is known of her fate after her transfer to the state hospital. She was still listed as an inmate in 1933, but Parks seems to have disappeared from public sight shortly thereafter, and no records have been found stating that she was either released or spent her final days incarcerated. To date, no one ever learned what prompted her to commit such heinous crimes rather than simply return Dorothy and Timothy Rogers to their father. As the fate of at least four missing children remains unknown to this day, perhaps an enigmatic disappearance is a fitting conclusion to her story.

The Sphinx Woman

About the Author

Patricia A. Martinelli, M.A., is the curator of the Vineland Historical and Antiquarian Society, the oldest local historical society in New Jersey. She is the author of nine books on regional history, including *New Jersey Ghost Towns*, *True Crime: New Jersey*, and *The Fantastic Castle of Vineland*.

Endnotes

1. In 1927, Margaret Lilliendahl, a Vineland housewife, was charged with arranging the murder of her husband in order to continue an affair with her lover, Willis Beach. The trial was a sensation and both Lilliendahl and Beach were found guilty of voluntary manslaughter.
2. "Gladys May Parks in First Ordeal," *The Altoona Mirror* (Altoona, PA), January 15, 1930, 18; "Revenge, Motive Hint, at Trial of Parks Woman," *Chester Times* (Chester, PA), January 15, 1930, 1; "'Midnight May' Goes on Trial," *Cincinnati Post*, January 13, 1930, 8.
3. Stone Woman: "Alleged Baby Killer Breaks Down at Grave She Dug for Little Tot," *Telegraph-Herald and Times Journal* (Dubuque, IA), November 11, 1929, 1–2. Iron Woman: "Iron Woman Sentenced to Twenty-Five Years in Jail," *The Frederick Post* (Frederick, MD), January 25, 1930, 1.
4. "Dead Babe's Dad to Help Woman at Murder Trial," *Daily News* (New York, NY), January 13, 1930, 3.
5. Park's twelve-page statement, given to Newark Police upon her surrender, and which provides many details of her life and crime, was widely reprinted, for example: "Alleged Baby Killer Breaks Down at Grave She Dug for Little Tot," *Dubuque Telegraph Herald and Times Journal* (Dubuque, IA), November 11, 1929, 1–2.
6. Ibid.
7. On the second day of the trial, one reporter noted "A narrow gold band, a wedding ring, was evident on the third finger of her left hand," "Murder Shovel Shown Parks Jury," *Reading Times* (Reading, PA), January 15, 1930, 7.
8. "Believes Both His Children Dead Now," *Boston Herald*, November 7, 1929, 2.
9. "Woman Confesses," *The Daily News* (Huntingdon, PA), November 11, 1929, 4; "Father, Witness in Murder Trial," *The Boston Herald*, January 15, 1930, 15.
10. The letter from Parks to Rogers, read during the trial, alludes to Rogers' visits to neighbors: "Gladys May Parks Near Faint as Tots' Father Tells Story," *Reading Times* (Reading, PA), January 15, 1930, 1.
11. *The Morning Call* (Allentown, PA), November 11, 1929, 1.
12. "Gladys Baker Admits N. J. Skeleton Murder; Reveals Boy's Body," *The Philadelphia Inquirer*, November 11, 1929, 4.
13. "Woman Admits Using Children For Blackmail," *The Tucaloosa News* (Tuscaloosa, FL), November 11, 1929, 3; "Alleged Baby Killer Breaks Down at Grave She Dug for Little Tot," *Dubuque Telegraph Herald and Times Journal* (Dubuque, IA), November 11, 1929, 1–2.
14. "Alleged Baby Killer Breaks Down at Grave She Dug for Little Tot," *Dubuque Telegraph Herald and Times Journal* (Dubuque, IA), November 11, 1929, 1–2.
15. Ibid.
16. "Women Attempt To Lynch Accused Slayer of Babies," *San Antonio Express*, November 12, 1929, 1. See also "Gladys May Parks Was under Severe Gruelling," *Lebanon Daily News* (Lebanon, PA), November 12, 1929, 11.
17. "Alleged Baby Killer Breaks Down at Grave She Dug for Little Tot," *Dubuque Telegraph Herald and Times Journal* (Dubuque, IA), November 11, 1929, 1–2.
18. Ibid.
19. *The Miami News* (Miami, FL), November 17, 1929, 32.
20. One newsman described Parks undergoing "140 hours of almost continuous inquisition," Frank W. Griffin, "Court Curtain Rises on Mrs. Parks' Battle for Her Life Tomorrow," *Sunday Courier-Post* (Camden, NJ), January 12, 1930, 3.
21. "Everybody Lying but Her, Gladys Parks Indicates," *The Sandusky Star-Journal* (Sandusky, OH), November 14, 1929, 10.
22. Ibid.
23. "N. J. Woman is Guarded from Mobs," *Danville Bee* (Danville, VA), November 12, 1929, 1.
24. *The Morning Call* (Allentown, PA), November 11, 1929, 1.
25. "Death of Children is Laid to Woman," *The Helena Daily Independent* (Helena, MO), November 11, 1929, 1–2.
26. "Woman Admits Using Children for Blackmail," *The Morning Herald* (Hagerstown, MD), November 11, 1929, 1, 12.
27. "Woman Confesses," *The Daily News* (Huntingdon, PA), November 11, 1929, 4.
28. The best review of the first day of the trial, which established many of the details of both children's death, is found in "Sphinx Woman Calm at Death Demand," *The Morning Post* (Camden, NJ), January 14, 1930, 6, 15.
29. "Gladys May Parks Weeps and Sleeps at Trial," *Reading Times* (Reading, PA), January 14, 1930, 1. The press was fascinated with Parks' appearance; here her apparel is described on the second day of the trial: "Mrs. Parks yesterday had discarded the somber black dress she wore on the opening day of the trial. She wore a green silk dress with a wide white collar and cuffs, flesh-colored hose and black shoes": "Gladys May Parks in first Ordeal," *The Altoona Mirror* (Altoona, PA), January 15, 1930, 18.
30. "Gladys May Parks on Trial for Life," *Reading Times* (Reading, PA), January 14, 1930, 2.
31. "Gladys Parks Takes Stand to Free Self," *Somerset Daily Herald* (Somerset, PA), January 18, 1930, 1.
32. "Gladys May Parks Retracts Charge," *Reading Times* (Reading, PA), January 18, 1930, 4.
33. Ibid.
34. "Gladys Parks is Given 25 Years in Baby Murders," *Chester Times* (Chester, PA), January 20, 1930, 1.
35. "Gladys May Parks Taken from Prison to Insane Asylum," *The Morning News* (Wilmington, DE), August 30, 1930, 1.
36. "Murderer of Two Children Is Committed to State Hospital," *Evening Times* (Vineland, NJ), August 30, 1930, 1.

A Recent SJCHC Publication

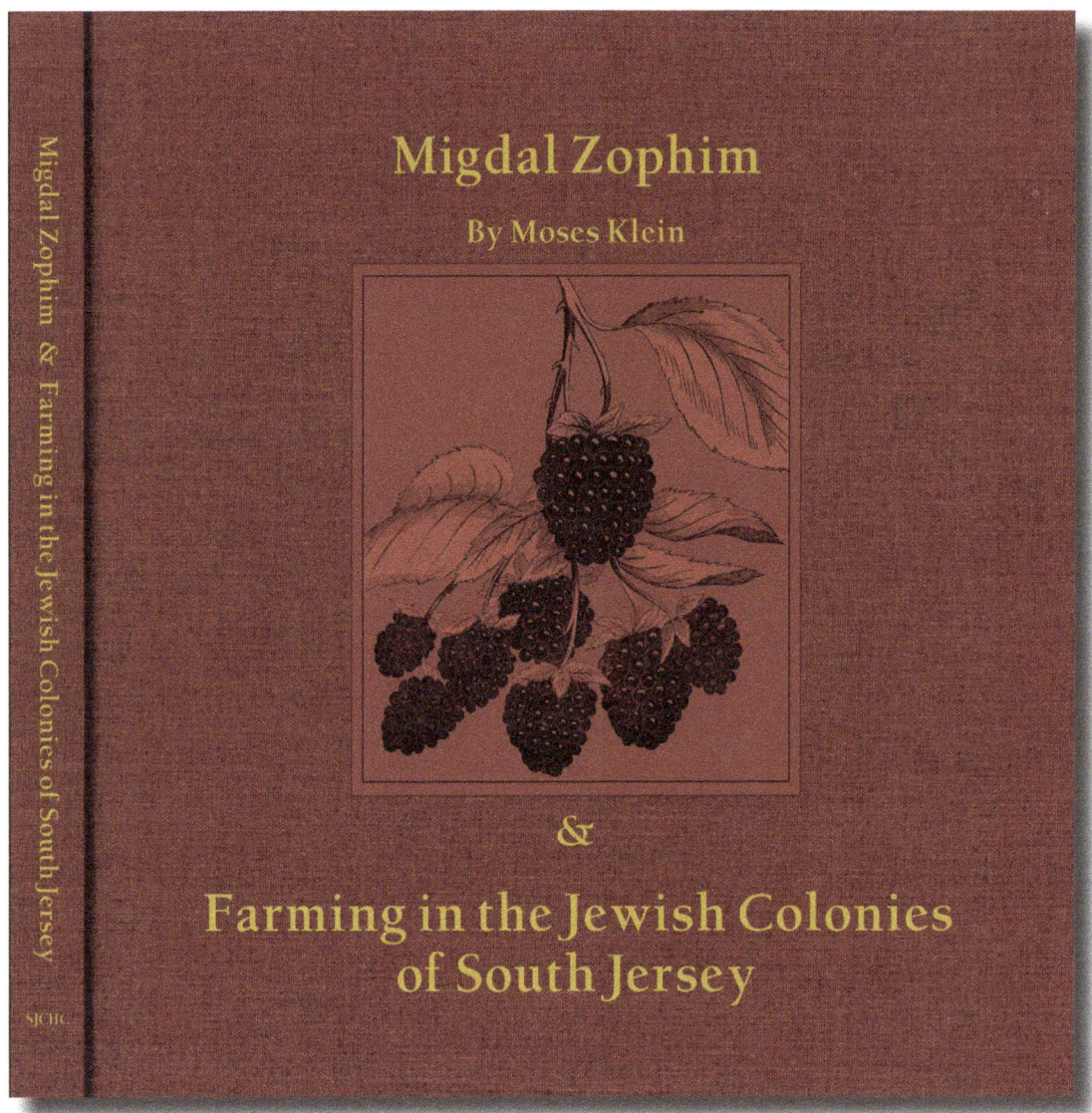

In 1889, Moses Klein published *Migdal Zophim*, a collection of essays that offers farming—in both Palestine and New Jersey—as a solution to the crisis of Jews fleeing Eastern European persecution. This republication supplements Klein's historical work with twenty additional accounts of the New Jersey farming colonies of Alliance, Rosenhayn, and Carmel, dating from 1882 to 1907. Twenty original photographs have been reproduced along with twenty-three additional photographs not printed in the first edition. Read descriptions of South Jersey's Jewish farming colonies as voiced by the early settlers and their contemporaries.

Migdal Zophim & Farming in the Jewish Colonies of South Jersey.
ISBN: 978-1-947889-89-7. Paperback; pagination, xxii + 266; with index; $19.95.

Horseshoe Crabs:
Ancient Migrators

Kenneth W. Able, Thomas M. Grothues, and Paola López-Duarte

As the sea level has risen over the last 10,000 to 12,000 years, and estuaries and barrier islands have migrated from offshore to their present locations, horseshoe crabs have continued to migrate with the estuaries. During this time, horseshoe crabs likely became apparent to the Lenni Lenape Indians in the Mullica Valley when the adult horseshoe crabs migrated onto sandy beaches to spawn as they do today (Fig. 1).[1] The Lenape and subsequent European settlers incorporated them into agriculture as fertilizer,[2] and this continued into the twentieth century, especially along Delaware Bay shores, where they are abundant (Fig. 2). Subsequently the adults, and especially the females, were used as bait for trapping American eels and conch, as well as in the biomedical industry. For the latter, *Limulus* amoebocyte lysate is extracted from their blood cells to identify disease-causing bacteria.[3] Over this history, they have even been considered as human food.[4] In recent years, estuarine ecologists and ornithologists have recognized the importance of evaluating the interactions between oyster aquaculture and horseshoe crab spawning beaches,[5] the role of horseshoe crab eggs as a food source for shorebirds and fish,[6] and other critical roles in estuarine ecosystems.[7] These studies have strongly influenced the conservation and management of this species.[8]

Figure 1. Adult horseshoe crabs spawning on the beach with numerous laughing gulls feeding on the eggs.

These ancient relatives of spiders predate dinosaurs on earth. They match their distribution to the needs of the different life history stages in the present-day Mullica Valley. The adults are residents on the continental shelf off New Jersey from fall through spring,[9] when they are feeding extensively.[10] However, the eggs require well oxygenated environments and relatively quiet sandy beaches; estuaries provide both of these as they are buffered from large waves in these protected areas.[11] In addition, the beaches are warm in summer, thus providing the appropriate temperatures for the development of the eggs. To get to these beaches, the adults must migrate from the inner continental shelf to shallow estuaries (Fig. 3), including in Great Bay and Little Egg Harbor, based on our observations (Fig. 4). Once the eggs hatch, the larvae resemble the adults in miniature, but without a tail (Fig. 5). The hatched larvae can last in the first trilobite stage from two weeks to a year if they remain buried in

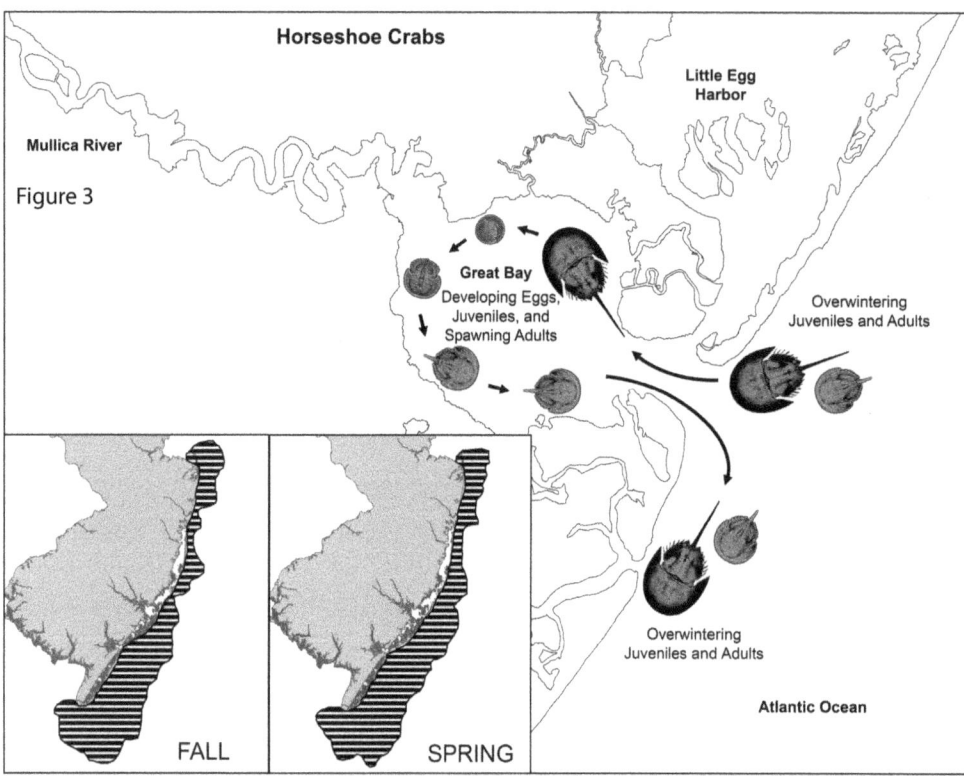

Figure 2. Horseshoe crabs stored on Warren's Landing on the St. Jones River, Delaware, 1928. The crabs nearest the scow have just been unloaded. Those behind the men have been stacked in rows to shed rainwater (from Shuster 2003). For many years, Delaware Bay was the only location that netted King or Horseshoe crabs for commercial purposes. The captured crustaceans underwent drying in a furnace and then were ground in a steam-powered grinding mill and mixed with sodium sulfate. Farmers, particularly fruit growers, would purchase the resultant product, known as cancerine. Fertilizer dealers also bought it for further processing. Chicken and hog farmers attempted to use Horseshoe crab in their animal feed, but the meat developed a foul taste and the practice soon ended. Goshen, New Jersey, near Cape May, had the largest processing factory.

Figure 3. Location of different life history stages of the horseshoe crab as they occur in the Mullica Valley and the adjacent ocean. Overwintering adults (and juveniles) are found on the inner continental shelf in depths less than 90 ft. In the spring, the adults migrate inshore and spawn in the adjacent Great Bay and Little Egg Harbor estuaries. The eggs develop in the sand of the spawning beach, hatch out, and occur in the water column before settling to the bottom at the trilobite stage and continue to molt until they reach a size that enables them to migrate offshore. They remain on the inner shelf until they reach sexual maturity. At this stage, they will eventually migrate inshore to start the life cycle over again. Inset indicates the general distribution of large juveniles and adults on the adjacent inner continental shelf in fall and spring.

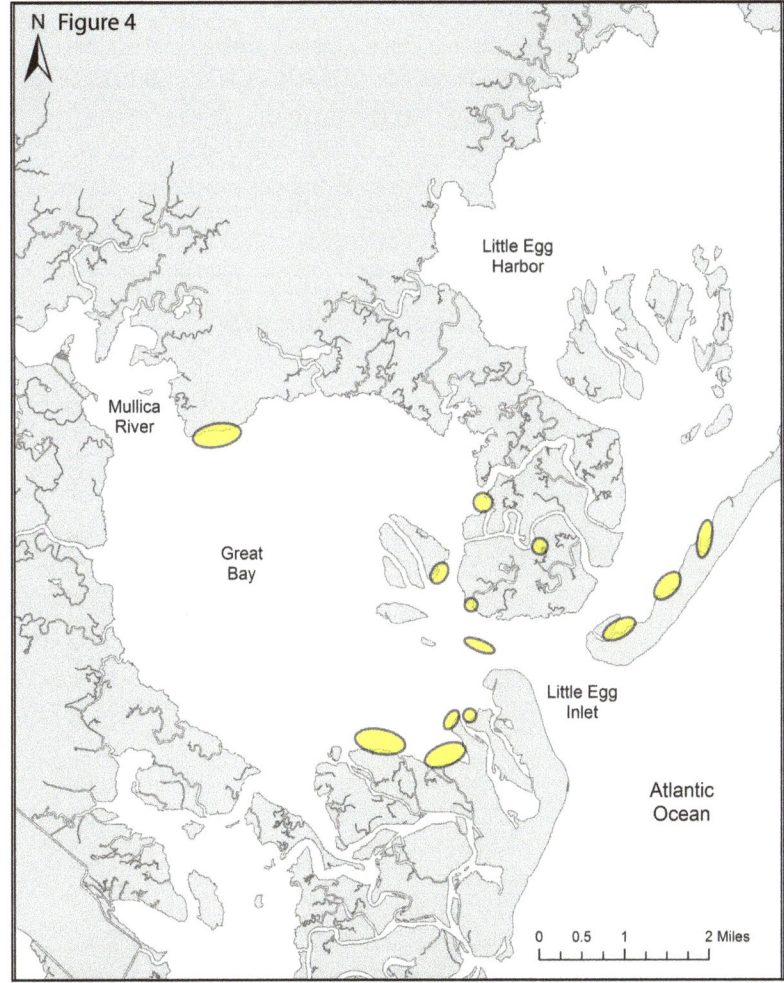

Figure 4. Known horseshoe crab spawning areas in Great Bay and Little Egg Harbor.

the sand and are not exposed to waves.[12] Our long-term sampling at the bridge over Little Sheepshead Creek, between Great Bay and Little Egg Harbor, indicates that the spring and early summer spawning results in the larvae being in the water column during June through September, with a peak in July (Fig. 6). Each individual only spends a short time in mid-water, at sizes of one eighth of an inch in width, before they settle to the bottom, molt and begin living there as juveniles (Fig. 7).

Unfortunately, we know little of the natural history of horseshoe crab juveniles relative to what is known about juveniles of many estuarine fishes.[13] One reason why we know less about horseshoe crabs is because, as juveniles, they spend a considerable amount of time buried in the substrate. Our laboratory observations in tanks with sand bottoms indicate they can bury as deep as one and a half inches, but with an average close to one third of an inch. Even this is deep enough for nets of all kinds to be pulled over their bodies without capturing them. In an effort to overcome this limitation, we have sampled into the bottom with a hydraulic dredge that allows us to pump the substrate onto a boat and separate them from the substrate in which they are living (Fig. 8). In these instances, we often capture the molts as well, an indication that they recently settled to the bottom from the water column.

In our collections in Great Bay and Little Egg Harbor, they can be found up to about four inches in width, most often in the lower estuary, where salinities are higher and in areas that are often protected from large scale wave action. Typically, the substrate in these nurseries is sandy and they remain buried much of the time. When they do come out of the sand, they can be captured in push nets over the bottom (Fig. 9). Several studies suggest that as they grow, larger juveniles are found deeper in estuaries.[14] Eventually, still as juveniles, they move from the estuary to the coastal ocean. These juveniles, now slightly larger than four inches, move into the adjacent shallow ocean primarily in the fall and stay in inshore water of less than 60 feet until they

Figure 5. Recently hatched horseshoe crab larvae (right) and small juvenile with tail (left) from laboratory rearing.

become sexually mature. Once they become mature, the males and females occur in similar depths in the ocean, as deep as about 90 feet. Then they develop a pattern of ocean to estuary movements for spawning that is typical for this species in New Jersey and in many other areas of the Mid-Atlantic Bight over their life span of seventeen to nineteen years.[15] Migration back into

ACKNOWLEDGEMENTS

Many technicians at Rutgers University Marine Field Station assisted with field collections and tracking. Willy Burton loaned us the hydraulic dredge while sampling for juveniles. Several interns, supported by the NSF-REU program at Rutgers, assisted in related parts of this study.

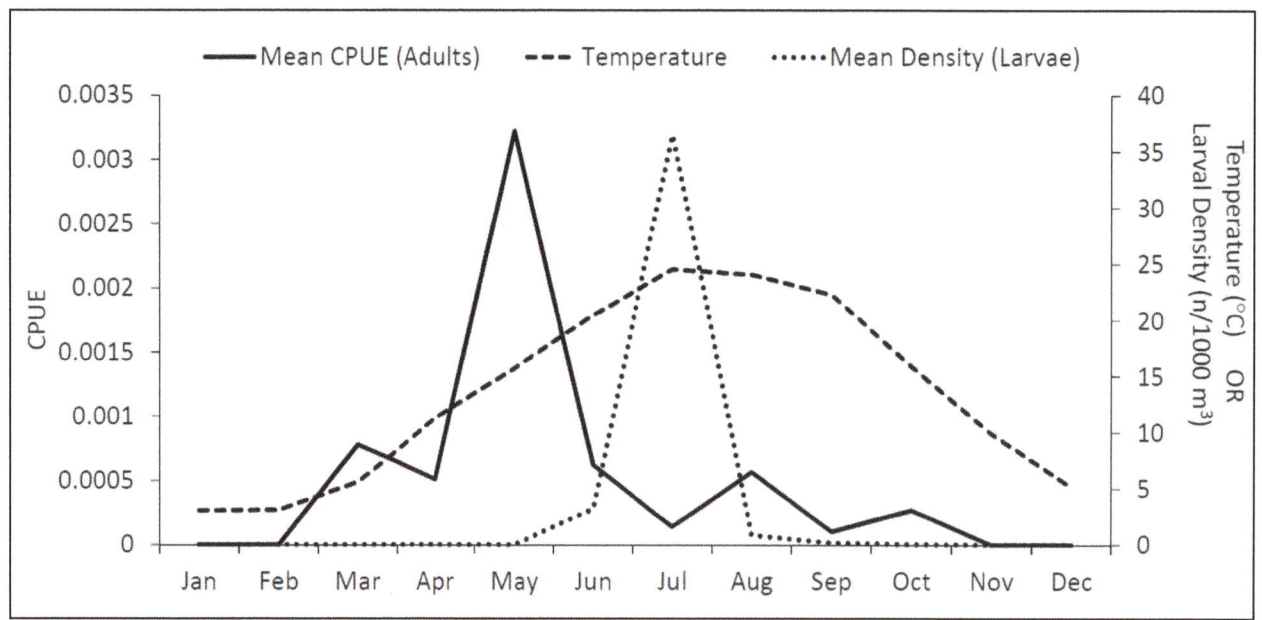

Figure 6. Mean catch per unit effort (CPUE) of adult (n=119) and mean density of larval (n=1,304) horseshoe crabs relative to mean temperature across months. Sampling took place at Little Sheepshead Creek (larvae) from 2005–2014 and in Great Bay and Little Egg Harbor estuaries (adults) from 1988–1990 and 1996–2015.

the estuary to spawn typically occurs in spring or early summer. We know this because we have followed their movements by placing acoustic tags on their shells (Fig. 10). This approach allows us to track crabs from boats at the surface, and we have learned that many adults leave the estuary for the ocean by July or August, while some remain in the estuary as late as September or October.

Now that we are uncovering how horseshoe crabs use different habitats, we may have an increased ability to conserve and manage these populations. This is critical, given the importance of horseshoe crabs to portions of coastal ecosystems, migratory birds, and humans that use them for bait and in the biomedical industry, all of which are evident in southern New Jersey.

Figure 7. Juvenile horseshoe crabs found buried in sandy intertidal beaches in Little Egg Harbor at the southern end of Long Beach Island.

About the Authors

Ken Able is a Distinguished Professor in the Department of Marine and Coastal Sciences and the Director of the Rutgers University Marine Field Station. His interests are diverse and include the life history and ecology of fishes and other estuarine fauna, with an emphasis on habitat quality.

Tom Grothues is an Associate Research Professor in the Department of Marine and Coastal Sciences. His interests include the ecology of marine fish and crabs and the development of ways to study them.

Paola López-Duarte is an Assistant Professor in the Department of Biological Sciences at the University of North Carolina–Charlotte and was previously based at the Rutgers University Marine Field Station. Her primary research interests focus on the behavior and ecology of invertebrates and fish, especially the factors controlling larval dispersal, transport, and recruitment to adult habitats.

This article is part of an upcoming book by the senior author on the underwater natural history of the Mullica Valley.

Endnotes

1 G. Kreamer and S. Michels, "History of Horseshoe Crab Harvest on Delaware Bay," *Biology and Conservation of Horseshoe Crabs* (New York: Springer, 2009), 299–313.
2 C. N Shuster Jr., "King Crab Fertilizer: A Once-Thriving Delaware Bay Industry," *The American Horseshoe Crab*

Figure 8. Collecting small juvenile horseshoe crabs with hydraulic dredge that pumps the substrate and crabs to a boat, where they can be sorted, identified, and measured.

Figure 9. Pushnetting for larger juvenile horseshoe crabs.

Figure 10. Tom Grothues tagging adult horseshoe crabs (top) with close-up of mounted tag (bottom).

(Cambridge, MA: Harvard University Press, 2003), 341–57.

3 J. Berkson and C. N. Shuster Jr., "The Horseshoe Crab: The Battle for a True Multiple-Use Resource," *Fisheries* 24 (1999): 6–12. J. Levin, H. D. Hochstein, and T. J. Novitsky, "Clotting Cells and Limulus Amebocyte Lysate: An amazing Analytical Tool," *The American Horseshoe Crab* (Cambridge, MA: Harvard University Press, 2003), 310–40. T. J. Novitsky, "Biomedical Applications of Limulus Amebocyte Lysate," *Biology and Conservation of Horseshoe Crabs* (New York: Springer, 2009), 315–29.

4 Alan Davidson, *North Atlantic Seafood* (New York: The Viking Press, 1979).

5 D. Munroe, D. Bushek, P. Woodruff, and L. Calvo, "Intertidal Rack-and-Bag Oyster Farms Have Limited Interaction with Horseshoe Crab Activity in New Jersey, USA," *Aquaculture Environment Interactions* 9: 205–11.

6 M. L. Botton and B. A. Harrington, "Synchronies in Migration: Shorebirds, Horseshoe Crabs, and Delaware Bay," *The American Horseshoe Crab* (Cambridge, MA: Harvard University Press, 2003), 5–26. D. M. Nemerson and K. W. Able, "Spatial Patterns in Diet and Distribution of Juveniles of Four Fish Species in Delaware Bay Marsh Creeks: Factors Influencing Fish Abundance," *Marine Ecology Progress,* series 276 (2004):249-62. D. M. Nemerson and K. W. Able, "Juvenile Sciaenid Fishes Respond Favorably to Marsh Restoration in Delaware Bay," *Ecological Engineering* 25 (2005): 260–74.

7 M. L. Botton, R. E. Loveland, and A. Tiwari, "Distribution, Abundance, and Survivorship of Young-of-the-Year in a Commercially Exploited Population of Horseshoe Crabs Limulus polyphemus," *Marine Ecology Progress*, series 265 (2003): 175–84.

8 Shuster, "King Crab Fertilizer," 341–57. D. R. Smith, H. J. Brockmann, M. A. Beekey, T. L. King, M. J. Millard, and J. Zaldívar-Rae, "Conservation Status of the American Horseshoe Crab, (Limulus polyphemus): A Regional Assessment," *Reviews in Fish Biology and Fisheries* 27 (2017): 135–75.

9 K. W. Able, P. López-Duarte, T. M. Grothues, L. Barry, R. Petrecca, J. Fredricks, C. Navara, and A. Hanson, in press. "Horseshoe Crabs (Limulus polyphemus) Habitats in a Small Estuary and the Adjacent Inner Continental Shelf: Linkages Across Mid-Atlantic Bight Seascapes," *Northeastern Naturalist*.

10 Shuster, "King Crab Fertilizer," 341–57.

11 L. I. Anderson and C. N. Shuster Jr., "Throughout Geologic Time: Where Have They Lived?" *The American Horseshoe Crab* (Cambridge, MA: Harvard University Press, 2003): 189–223.

12 C. N. Shuster and K. H. Sekiguchi, "Growing Up Takes About Ten Years and Eighteen Stages," *The American Horseshoe Crab* (Cambridge, MA: Harvard University Press, 2003): 103–32.

13 K. W. Able, "Natural History: An Approach Whose Time Has Come, Passed, and Needs to Be Resurrected," *ICES Journal of Marine Science* 73, no. 9 (2016): 2150–155. doi:10.1093/icesjms/fsw049.

14 A. Rudloe. "Aspects of the Biology of Juvenile Horseshoe Crabs, Limulus polyphemus," *Bulletin of Marine Science* 31 (1981): 125–133. D. R. Smith, H. J. Brockmann, M. A. Beekey, T. L. King, M. J. Millard, and J. Zaldívar-Rae, "Conservation Status of the American Horseshoe Crab, (Limulus polyphemus): A Regional Assessment," *Reviews in Fish Biology and Fisheries* 27 (2017): 135–75. M. L. Botton, R. E. Loveland, and A. Tiwari, "Distribution, Abundance, and Survivorship of Young-of-the-Year in a Commercially Exploited Population of Horseshoe Crabs Limulus polyphemus," *Marine Ecology Progress,* series 265 (2003): 175–84. R. H. Carmichael, D. Rutecki, I. Valiela, "Abundance and Population Structure of the Atlantic Horseshoe Crab Limulus polyphemus in Pleasant Bay, Cape Cod," *Marine Ecology Progress*, series 246 (2003): 225–39. W. H. Burton. "Distribution of Juvenile Horseshoe Crabs in Subtidal Habitats of Delaware Bay Using a Suction-Dredge Sampling Device," *Biology and Conservation of Horseshoe Crabs* (New York: Springer, 2009): 285–93.

15 Shuster, "King Crab Fertilizer," 341–57. Shuster Sekiguchi, "Growing Up Takes About Ten Years and Eighteen Stages," 103–32. The *Mid-Atlantic Bight* is the coastal region running from Massachusetts to North Carolina.

All Aboard for Amatol, New Jersey

Daniel J. Dinnebeil

As a result of America's entry into World War I on April 6, 1917, Atlantic County received a great expansion of its industrial economic base. Among the largest results of this expansion was the construction of Amatol, a planned shell-loading munitions plant and workers' village that once occupied a tract of 6,000 acres between East Hammonton and Elwood. Amatol and other World War I inspired construction efforts, such as Camp Dix in Burlington County, are fascinating, in part due to the rapidity of their construction. In just nine months' time, the new town and manufactory at Amatol were completed and reached a population of 7,000. Today, the Pine Barrens have all but reclaimed the former site of Amatol.

History

The history of Amatol began in December 1917 with the incorporation of the Atlantic Loading Company.[1] Acting under the aegis of the United States government, the Atlantic Loading Company received contracts to construct a large munitions plant and an accompanying town to house workers. In early 1918, the Atlantic Loading Company had initially planned to build the munitions plant and town near Camp Dix, but the war department had concerns over water pollution and the safety of the camp's personnel, and told the contractor to locate elsewhere.[2] In testimony given regarding Amatol, Lieutenant Colonel R. H. Hawkins stated that Camp Dix was not selected "because the commanding

THE RESPONSE TO THE CALL FOR SPEED

To the left, a work crew newly arrived in the South Jersey Pine Barrens, March 4, 1918, prepares to commence construction of Amatol, the World War I shell-loading facility and workers' town near Hammonton, New Jersey. The manufacturing plant was first built and loading operations began in July 1918. To the right is a street within the completed workers' town built and in use nine months later. From Victor F. Hammel, *Construction and Operation of a Shell Loading Plant and the Town of Amatol*, New Jersey, 4.

The 75 mm shell loading plant, Amatol. From Hammel, *Amatol*, 4.

officer of Camp Dix told us he did not want it near his soldiers."[3]

Other sites considered included Toms River, Lakehurst, Lacey, and Hammonton.[4] Ultimately, Hammonton was selected. Although no definite source can be cited as to why the Hammonton-Mullica Township site was selected over the other three candidates, major reasons did include the potential quality of town life and the design of a safety zone. Additional testimony from Lieutenant Colonel Hawkins reveals this consideration: "We had to build rather attractive accommodations [at Amatol] . . . to get [people] there. . . . We had to make it just as attractive as we could in order to get people to stay there; particularly in view of the knowledge of most people of the danger."[5] Being situated between Atlantic City and Philadelphia, Amatol was conveniently located for ease of access to the Jersey Shore and a great metropolitan city. In addition to town amenities, Lieutenant Colonel Hawkins also explained that the size of Amatol—6,000 acres—was meant as a "substantial safety zone."[6]

Construction and Development

After the company made its final site determination, the Atlantic Loading Company immediately went to work, which caught neighboring towns by surprise. *The Tuckerton Beacon* reported that on March 2, 1918, the residents of Elwood and Hammonton went to bed with a quiet night as if it had been any other. To their surprise, they awoke to see a large force of strangers in their midst, a half hundred freight cars bearing the legend "Ordnance Department U.S.A.," and heavy motor trucks noisily chugging in the streets.[7] The next day, March 4, construction began.

A company street, Amatol. From Hammel, *Amatol*, 293.

All Aboard for Amatol

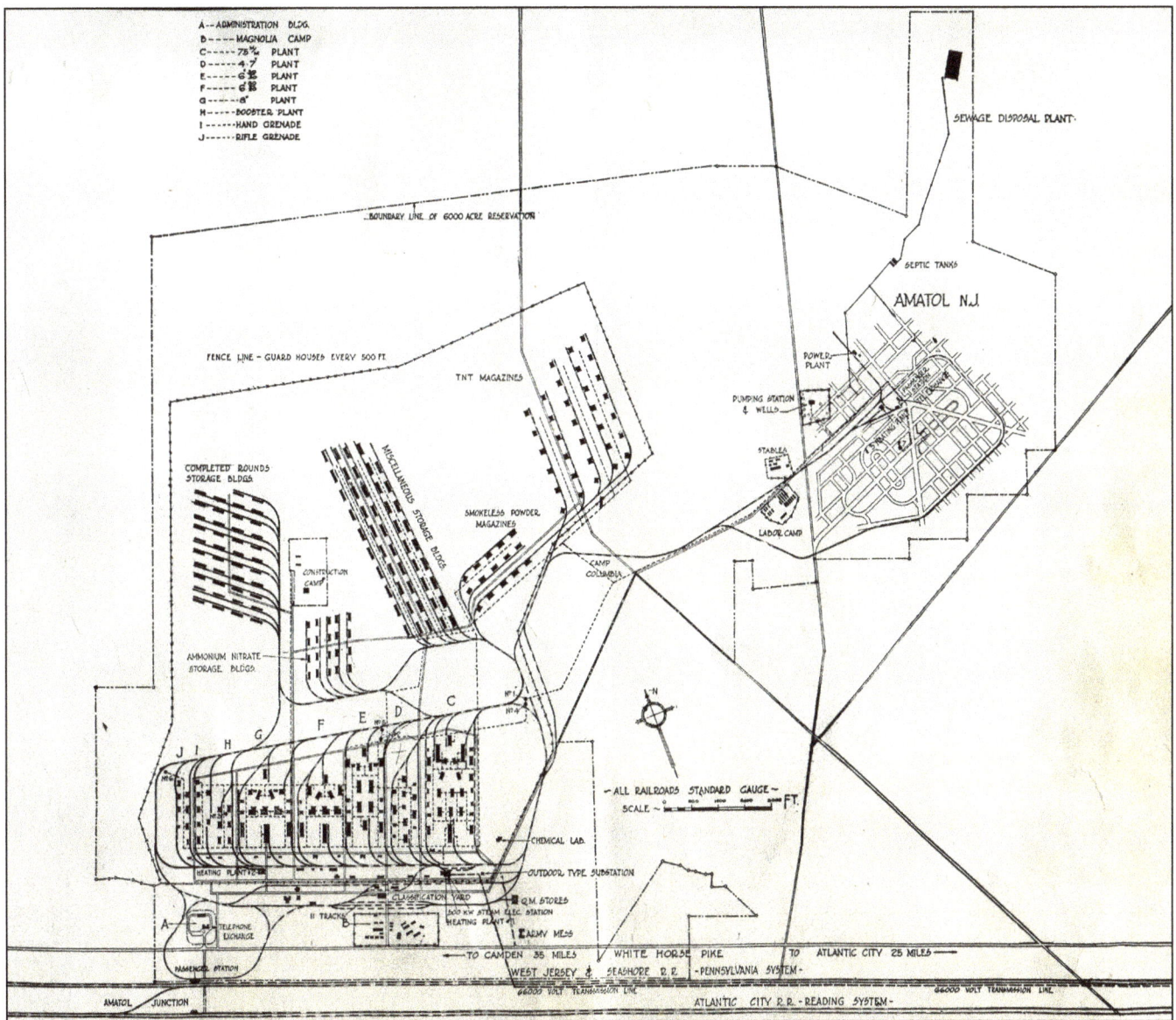

The Amatol facility occupied 6,000 acres. Above, the loading plant occupies the lefthand property. The workers' town is located upper right. "The magnitude of the work is indicated by the extent and variety of the utilities; three central steam heating stations, two auxiliary steam-electric generating stations, a 1,750,000 gallon water supply system, a modern sewage disposal system and ultimately 50 miles of standard gauge railroad with 10 locomotives and 30 passenger coaches." Quotation and image from Hammel, *Amatol*, 13.

In his work, *Construction and Operation of a Shell Loading Plant and the Town of Amatol, New Jersey*, commonly known as the "Amatol book," Victor F. Hammel records a description of the construction. In total, 1,600 acres had to be cleared for the plant, and 38 acres had to be cleared and 255 acres trimmed for the town.[8] This was no easy task. The land was mostly wooded with some acres of swamp and was difficult to clear due to the "dense, tangled nature of growth."[9] The initial workforce included 40 men, and, within the first week, the first bunkhouse and mess hall were built.[10]

Development was rapid. By June, the population was nearly 2,000, and train service was added.[11] By August, advertisements for Amatol described it as

a city with all modern improvements ... with electric lights, a fire department, a police department, a modern sewage system, a modern water plant, a theatre, a Y.M.C.A, an auditorium, bowling alleys, and other city amenities.[12]

Amatol also promised many employment opportunities, not just with the munitions plant, but with local businesses, like barbers, tailors, jewelers, watchmakers, and grocers.

By the signing of the armistice, plant and town structures included 122 loading buildings, 159 storage buildings and magazines, 4 administration buildings, 6 office buildings, 22 industrial buildings, 7 hospitals,

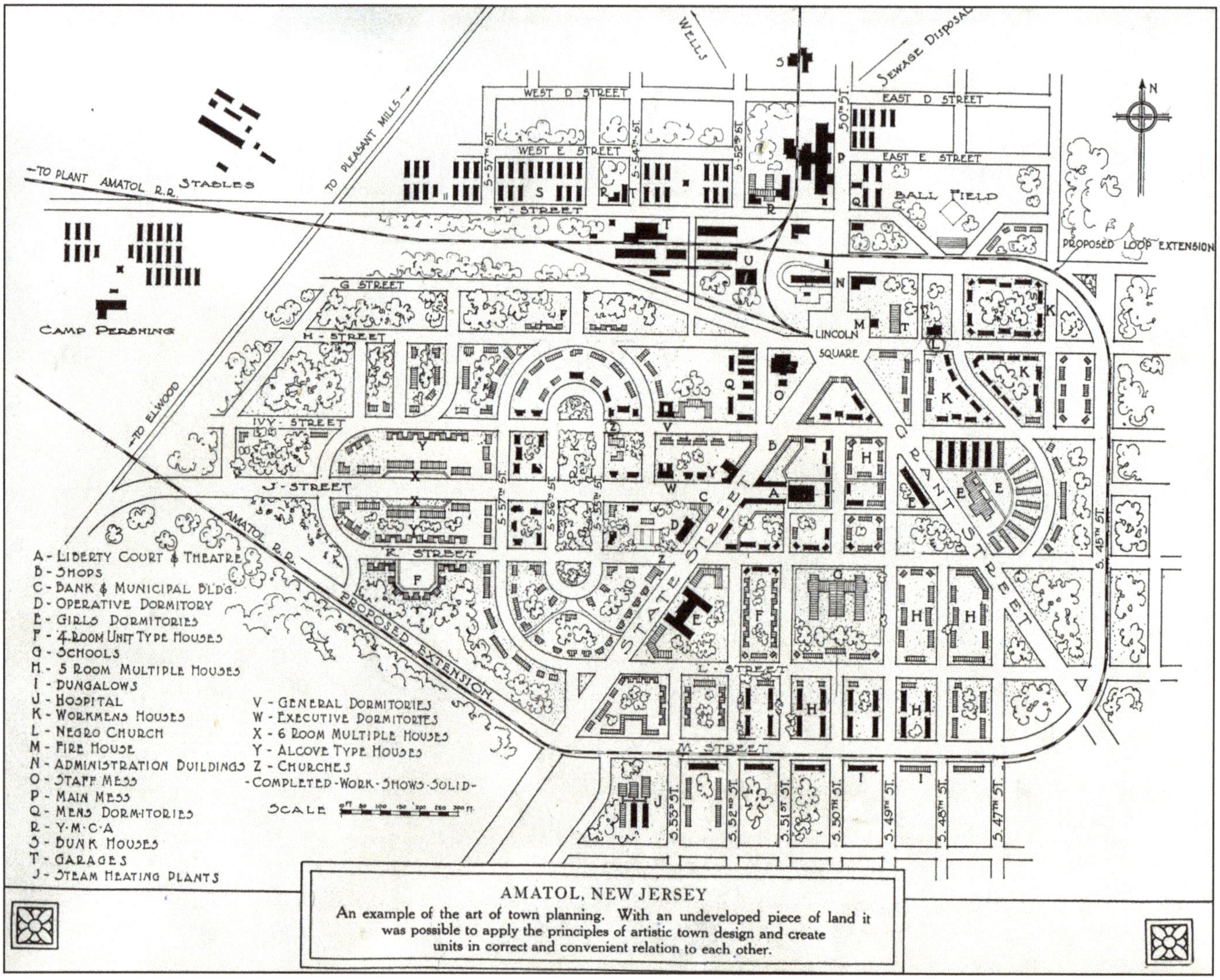

Amatol, New Jersey. "An example of the art of town planning. With an undeveloped piece of land it was possible to apply the principles of artistic town design and create units in correct and convenient relation to each other." Quotation and illustration from Hammel, *Amatol*, 179.

East K Street from Fiftieth Street, Amatol. Postcard courtesy of the Paul W. Schopp collection.

16 recreation centres, 1 theatre, 18 mess halls, 4 garages, 15 warehouses, 21 railroad structures, 12 stables, 130 guardhouses, sentry boxes, searchlights, etc., 21 commercial stores, 98 male dormitories and bunkhouses, 21 female dormitories, 140 miscellaneous buildings, 24 Army barracks, 4 Y.M.C.A.s, 11 individual residences, 33 multiple houses, 227 workmen's houses, 1 post office, 1 school house, 2 fire houses, 444 tent tops, 96 two-roomed family apartments, 179 four-roomed family apartments, and 23 three-roomed family apartments.[13] On average, there were four buildings built per day, which was a remarkable speed.[14] The final workforce included over 5,000 construction workers.[15]

The town reached a peak population of 7,000,[16] had the capacity to house over 10,000,[17] and was planned to accommodate a possible population of 25,000.[18]

Amatol Plant

Loading operations at the Amatol plant began on July 31, 1918, and, on August 3, the first shell was loaded.[19] The plant was capable of loading

> 60,000 shells of all sizes, 50,000 boosters, 50,000 hand grenades, and 20,000 rifle grenades per day, as well as components. To accomplish this work there were 15 smokeless-powder magazines, 33 T.N.T. magazines, 49 miscellaneous storage buildings, 642 plant structures in all.[20]

The plant, during its operational lifespan, loaded over 9,000,000 rounds of ammunition of various types and sizes.[21]

Although T.N.T. was preferred and used when available, amatol, a mixture of T.N.T. and ammonium nitrate, was used as an alternative due to the shortage of T.N.T. Amatol was "the main charge pressed into the shell (unless straight T.N.T. or a 50/50 mix was used), [and] contains 80 percent of ammonium nitrate and 20 percent of T.N.T."[22] The one disadvantage of amatol was that ammonium nitrate absorbs moisture rapidly, and, in time, deteriorates. The life of a shell loaded with amatol was uncertain after five years while the life of a shell loaded with T.N.T. was indefinite, and certainly at least 25 years.[23]

The Army's Ordnance Department took control of the plant in February 1919 and denoted it Amatol Arsenal.[24] By 1923, Amatol Arsenal ceased operations.

Camp Amatol

In October 1918, 2,400 troops arrived at Amatol to assist in operations there.[25] Their job was to bring the

(Top to bottom) General Dormitory; Interior Swimming Pool; Main Mess Hall; Bank Building and Post Office, Amatol. Postcards courtesy of the Paul W. Schopp collection.

(Top to bottom) Receiving empty shell for loading; the delicate process of pouring T.N.T. into shells; inserting boosters in 75 mm shells; (bottom left) painting completed rounds; (bottom right) placing completed shells in fibre containers in preparation for shipping. Photographs from Hammel, *Amatol*.

All Aboard for Amatol

(Top left) Guard train enroute to T.N.T. section; (top right) Battalion Roll Call; (middle) African American Road-Working Detachment; (bottom left) Canteen; (bottom right) Enlisted Men's Barracks. Photographs from Hammel, *Amatol*.

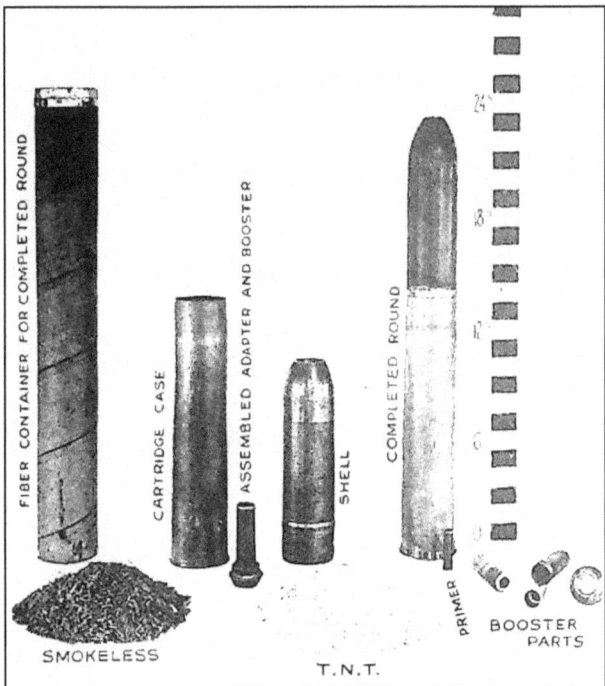

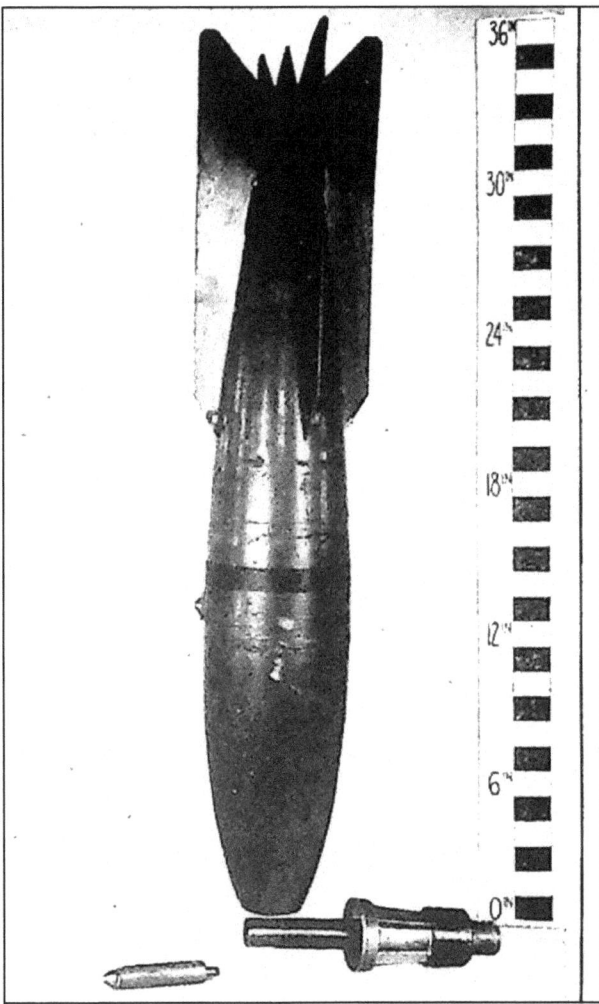

(Top) 75 mm shell component parts; (bottom) Mark III Drop Bomb. Both munitions were loaded at Amatol. Photographs from Hammel, *Amatol*.

output to full loading capacity and, when necessary, perform civilian tasks. *The Philadelphia Inquirer* reported that in mid October, many of these soldiers decided to take French leave—an unauthorized departure—by traveling to Atlantic City. A few of the soldiers were jailed when they were unable to show a proper pass for their "leave of absence."[26] By the time of the armistice, there were 3,800 officers and enlisted men at Camp Amatol, as it became known.[27]

There were also Camp Amatol sports teams. Basketball was a popular sport played amongst soldiers, including officers. A December 6, 1918, news article records, "the Hammonton five defeated the U.S. Ordnance quintet from Camp Amatol by the score of 19 to 10."[28] A December 13, 1918, article describes the U.S. Ordnance Officers team defeating the Amatol team in basketball by the score of 25 to 10.[29]

Conclusion

In just a matter of months after signing the Armistice, the civilian population of Amatol had virtually vanished, with only a few hundred remaining. The former munitions complex experienced a brief resurgence in 1926 after an investor backed the construction of the Atlantic City Speedway there. The revival was short-lived as interest quickly waned among the visiting public and other investors.

Little remains of Amatol today. After a hike through the Pine Barrens, remnants of the munitions plant, town, and racetrack can be found at the former site of Amatol. Of the many buildings and homes constructed, only two still remain: the now-abandoned State Police barracks outside of Hammonton and one house, which was moved to the White Horse Pike, where it is still occupied.[30] During the 1980s, the Amatol site was considered for use as a landfill, but the proposal was rejected due to environmental concerns and opposition by local residents.[31] Recently, in 2017, more than 500 acres of Amatol (now the Pine Barrens) were preserved.[32]

Amatol was not the only planned community that South Jersey saw built during World War I. Belcoville, Atlantic County, was also built as a munitions plant and village. Yorkship Village (now Fairview), Camden County, was built to house shipyard workers and their families. In addition, America also saw many new military bases built, which included Camp Dix (now Fort Dix), Burlington County.

What was the overall impact of Amatol on the surrounding area? There is no reliable and readily-available information to answer this question. Where did the residents of Amatol go once operations ceased? According

(Left to right) Attractive worker's home with enclosed porch and sun parlor; Corner of a typical living room; Four-room two-family cottage. Photographs from Hammel, *Amatol*, 189, 195.

to the *Press of Atlantic City*, "Many of Amatol's laborers, predominantly Irish and Polish from Philadelphia, stayed in the area and started families."[33]

As the centennial of America's participation in the First World War draws to a close, it is good to take a moment to remember a significant town, built in a forest in New Jersey, which contributed to the war effort and provided employment for thousands of American workers.

Postcard photograph of private Joseph Straley, Military Police, Amatol, New Jersey. Courtesy of the Paul W. Schopp collection.

About the Author

Daniel J. Dinnebeil completed his Master of Arts in American Studies at Stockton University in Fall 2018. He also received his BA in Economics from Stockton in 2015. Having served in the United States Coast Guard as an Electronics Technician, Daniel has an abiding interest in military history.

Endnotes

1. Victor F. Hammel, *Construction and Operation of a Shell-Loading Plant and the Town of Amatol, New Jersey: For the United States Government Ordnance Department, U.S. Army* (New York: Atlantic Loading Company, 1918), 14.
2. "Locate War Plant at Toms River," *Asbury Park Press*, February 21, 1918.
3. *War Expenditures: Hearings Before Subcommittee No. 5 (Ordnance) of the Select Committee on Expenditures in the War Department, House of Representatives, Sixty-sixth Congress on War Expenditures*, vol. 1 (Washington: Government Printing Office, 1919), 491.
4. "Locate War Plant at Toms River," *Asbury Park Press*, February 21, 1918.
5. *War Expenditures*, 511.
6. *War Expenditures*, 493.
7. "People Arise to Discover Evidence of Government's War Activities," *Tuckerton Beacon*, March 7, 1918.
8. Hammel, *Construction and Operation*, 16.
9. Ibid.
10. Ibid.
11. "Accommodations for Loaders," *Philadelphia Inquirer*, June 5, 1918.
12. "Amatol [Advertisement]," *Philadelphia Inquirer*, August 25, 1918.
13. Hammel, *Construction and Operation*, 17–18.
14. Ibid., 18.
15. Ibid., 25.
16. *Forty-Third Annual Report of the Department of Health of the State of New Jersey* (Trenton: MacCrellish & Quigley, 1912) 175.
17. Hammel, *Construction and Operation*, 16
18. Ibid., 181.
19. Ibid., 16.

20 *The Ordnance Districts, 1918–1919* (Washington: Government Printing Office, 1920), 110.
21 Hammel, *Construction and Operation*, 61.
22 Ibid., 135.
23 Ibid., 136.
24 *War Department, Annual Reports, 1919* (Washington: Government Printing Office, 1920), 3937.
25 "Troops Taking Over Loading Plant," *Philadelphia Inquirer*, October 10, 1918.
26 "3000 Soldiers Reach Shell Loading Plants: Scores Take French Leave and Visit Seaside Resort, Housing Problem," *Philadelphia Inquirer*, October 14, 1918.
27 *The Ordnance Districts, 1918–1919* (Washington: Government Printing Office, 1920), 111.
28 "Hammonton Defeats Ordnance Five," *Philadelphia Inquirer*, December 6, 1918.
29 *Philadelphia Inquirer*, December 13, 1918.
30 Wallace McKelvey, "Mullica Township Ghost Town Amatol was Once Munitions Village," *Press of Atlantic City*, December 16, 2013.
31 McKelvey, "Mullica Township Ghost Town Amatol."
32 Michelle Brunetti, "Mullica's Amatol Site Part of Recent Preservation in Pinelands," *Press of Atlantic City*, October 14, 2017.
33 McKelvey, "Mullica Township Ghost Town Amatol."

Despite Hammel's volume describing the above view as the junction where Camden, Atlantic City, and Amatol Railroad trains meet, this view shows one of the two wyes on Atlantic Loading Company property at the northern end of the loop track extending northward from the West Jersey & Seashore (nee Camden & Atlantic) Railroad line. Both sides of the loop track crossed the White Horse Pike and enveloped the company's telephone exchange, based on the map included on page 47 of this article. The narrow wye throat suggests this is the westernmost wye at the top of the loop track. While the Atlantic Loading Company operated its own Amatol Railroad within the plant's confines, the West Jersey & Seashore carried virtually all of the freight to and from the loading facility. The Reading's Atlantic City Railroad also benefited from the increased passenger revenue as a result of its "Amatol" station. The wye track assemblage provided a convenient way to reverse the direction of an entire train. In this view, every leg of the wye features a passenger train, likely posed for photographic purposes. Photograph from Hammel, *Amatol*, 271.

Unlikely Farmers:
Tokens of the Allivine Canning Company

Todd R. Sciore

"Farming is a profession of hope"—Brian Brett

Numerous waves of immigrants have landed on American shores with little more than the clothes on their back, looking for a better life than the one they left behind. With cultures and traditions as varied as a patchwork quilt, many of them shared the common threads of agriculture and hope playing an important role in transitioning to their new homeland. The rise of small, rural Southern New Jersey communities such as Alliance, Norma, Rosenhayn, and Woodbine offered poor Eastern European Jewish immigrants the potential for a new life in The United States. These communities played essential roles in both Jewish and New Jersey history. Outside of dedicated academic and cultural circles, however, the circumstances and series of "firsts" surrounding their formation remain largely unknown.

While the farms either no longer exist, or are no longer owned by descendants of the original settlers, the story of Southern New Jersey's early Jewish immigrants remains an inspiring look at the trials and tribulations of adjusting not only to a new culture, but a new way of life. It was often the case that farming was not the immigrants previous occupation, and "the early settlers had to quickly learn to cope with difficult and primitive conditions."[1] To add a tangible, numismatic/exonumic aspect to their story are tokens of the Allivine Canning Company of Norma, New Jersey, an outgrowth of the first successful Jewish farm colony in America.

A plaque at historic Alliance Cemetery pays tribute to the area's Jewish settlers.

Immigration and Assimilation

Thousands of Jewish immigrants came to America during the late nineteenth century to escape "increasing anti-Semitism in Czarist Russia," and hundreds established Jewish farming communities throughout Southern New Jersey.[2] Ellen Eisenberg, an authority on these communities, notes that "the New Jersey colonies of Salem and Cumberland Counties . . . began as communal, agrarian settlements."[3] The colony of Alliance, however, abandoned the communal work system within a couple years, and "by 1884, the pattern of single family farming was established."[4] Eisenberg points out that the site for Alliance was chosen "because it was on the New Jersey Central rail line" and thus easily accessible from larger East Coast urban centers.[5]

Jews making the journey from Eastern Europe to America received assistance from more established Jewish communities as well as dedicated philanthropic organizations such as the Baron de Hirsch Fund, Jewish Agricultural Society and the Hebrew Immigrant Aid Society. Essentially the new arrivals "were under the close supervision of New York and Philadelphia sponsors" and while their close proximity "yielded tremendous benefits for the Alliance colony in monetary support, this support was not unconditional . . . and led to a high level of intervention."[6]

Farm lands at Alliance Colony. View from the Tiphereth Israel Synagogue. The original black and white image has been colorized. From Moses Klein, *Migdal Zophim* (Philadelphia: 1889).

To put it another way, the benefactors had goals in mind for the new arrivals—namely assimilation. They believed that "immigrants settled in rural areas would rapidly adopt American ways, for they would be surrounded by Americans rather than by other immigrants."[7] They also wanted to quickly wean the colonists off of charitable dependence and any lingering European socialist ideals by promoting independence and American style entrepreneurship. As Leonard G. Robinson noted in the 1912 publication *The Agricultural Activities of the Jews in America*, "Another institution which serves to promote the progress of Alliance is the cannery conducted by the Allivine Canning Company."[8]

Maurice Fels and Allivine Canning Company

Located in the small town of Norma, New Jersey, the Allivine Canning Company's name is an amalgam of the aforementioned town of Alliance and the nearby City of Vineland. The role of the canning company within the colony was best described by Robinson:

It was built in 1901 by Maurice Fels in cooperation with the Jewish Agricultural and Industrial Aid Society. This cannery affords a ready market for various products and has been an important factor in increasing the quantity and improving the quality of the products raised.[9]

Robinson's account is likely to be reliable as he served as the General Manager of the Jewish Agricultural and Industrial Aid Society in New York City.

As to the company's founder, Maurice Fels was a successful businessman and noted philanthropist. He was a member of the family behind Fels Naptha soap as well as the Fels Planetarium at The Franklin Institute in Philadelphia. "Because of their entrepreneurial success, the Fels could afford to be doers and givers on a grand scale."[10] He was a generous supporter of rural education initiatives and "subsidized many teachers, purchasing books for their personal and professional growth."[11] The citizens of Vineland even named a school after him.

Unlikely Farmers

The cannery reportedly paid fair prices and offered assistance in improving crop yields via selling them fertilizer "at cost" and "also provided farming practices lessons on its own model farm, and established lecture courses on agricultural topics."[12] Author Evelyn Bodek Rosen notes that "By 1908, Allivine Farm had become a part of the thriving Jewish farm life in South Jersey."[13] Author Mary B. Sim observed that

> The factory was well equipped with well-placed machinery and conditions of cleanliness were good.... Between 1916 and 1917, the factory had changed hands and at the latter date was reported as operated by F. A. Torsch, of the Torsch Packing Company.[14]

Inadvertently, this marked the beginning of the Jewish immigrant farmer's movement away from dependence on vegetable farming and eventually, as Rosen points out, "by the twenties and thirties, most of the farms began specializing in poultry..." and "after 1940 ... they left their farms for the cities."[15]

While I was unable to find out the exact location of the cannery, the existence of Can House Road seems to provide a reasonable clue, especially due to its close proximity to Alvine Road and Alliance Cemetery. Leonard Robinson's publication also notes that, in addition to Allivine, another cannery was built in 1912

... by the Jewish Agricultural and Industrial Aid Society ... in the immediate vicinity of Carmel. It provides the Jewish farmers of Carmel and Rosenhayn with a nearer market for their products.[16]

This second nearby cannery was noted as being leased to an experienced canner and operated as a private business.

Tokens

The two aluminum Allivine tokens pictured to the right have varying face values and feature slightly different wording as well. The smaller obverse of the 24mm specimen reads, "Allivine Company / Exchangeable / At The / Office / Of The / Company Only"; the reverse bears the denomination of "5." The 28mm specimen has a similar legend: "Exchangeable At The Office / Of The / Allivine / Co. / Only" on the reverse is the denomination "30." As neither piece notes that it is redeemable at a company store, I believe that they function like picker tickets, representing the

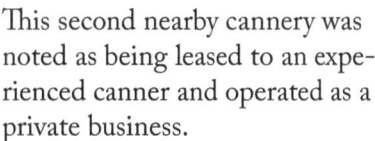

Allivine Canning Company, Norma, New Jersey. The factory's relatively new appearance suggests this view dates to between 1903 and 1908. Image courtesy of Marsha Levin Schumer for the Judge I. Harry Levin collection.

volume of work done. As such, they would have been exchangeable for pay as opposed to being actual compensation.

I welcome any additional information from readers. In particular, It would be of interest to find out whether the Ferracute Machine Company in nearby Bridgeton supplied any of Allivine's canning equipment.

As mentioned earlier in this article, the history of various Southern New Jersey Jewish farm settlements is, more likely than not, unknown to many local gentile residents. It would be disingenuous for me to not admit that, before writing this feature, I was one of them. Depending on which route I took to my office, I drove through the towns of Rosenhayn or Carmel daily for well over a decade but could not tell you one thing about their origin until I began conducting research for this article. I discovered that both were late nineteenth-century Jewish immigrant colonies. Ironically, if I took the route through Rosenhayn, I passed by Can House Road and Alvine Road whose names, until now, held little significance beyond marking the approximate halfway point to work. Such is the fun and allure of exonumia: in researching a pitted metal disc, you can get a history lesson about your own back yard.

Acknowledgment

I'd like to thank collector and author David Schenkman for kindly providing some cannery related research materials. The original version of this feature with different historical images was published in the January 2018 issue of *The Numismatist*, the official publication of The American Numismatic Association.

About the Author

Todd R. Sciore is a Stockton University graduate ('94) and is employed as Vice President & Commercial Lender with South Jersey based Newfield National Bank. Residing in Vineland, New Jersey, he has a general interest in National bank notes, tokens and merchant scrip from the South Jersey region. He has been published in *Coin World* and is a frequent contributor to *The Numismatist* as well as *South Florida Opulence* and its successor publications. His article "The Gettysburg Connection," in the July 2011 issue of *The Numismatist*, won a 2nd place Catherine Sheehan literary award. His article "Shinplasters," appeared in the first issue of *SoJourn*, spring 2016.

Endnotes

1. Ellen Eisenberg, *Jewish Agricultural Colonies in New Jersey, 1882–1920* (Syracause, NY: Syracuse University Press, 1995).
2. Leonard F. Vernon and Allen Meyers, *Jewish South Jersey* (Charleston, SC: Arcadia Publishing, 2007).
3. Eisenberg, *Jewish Agricultural Colonies in New Jersey*, 90.
4. Ibid, 97
5. Ibid, 98.
6. Ibid.
7. Ibid.
8. Leonard George Robinson, *The Agricultural Activities of the Jews in America* (New York: American Jewish Committee, 1912), 66.
9. Ibid.
10. Evelyn Bodek Rosen, *The Philadelphia Fels, 1880–1920: A Social Portrait* (Madison, NJ: Fairleigh Dickinson University Press, 2000), 20.
11. Ibid., 76.
12. Barbara Ellman, "Alliance, Norma and Brotmanville" (JewishGen KehilaLinks), https://kehilalinks.jewishgen.org/NJ_Farms/Alliance.html.
13. Rosen, *The Philadelphia Fels*, 74.
14. Mary B. Sim, *Commercial Canning in New Jersey History and Early Development* (Trenton: New Jersey Agricultural Society, 1951), 417.
15. Rosen, *The Philadelphia Fels*, 76.
16. Robinson, *The Agricultural Activities of the Jews in America*, 66.

Calling for Authors

Dear Readers,

You are perusing the sixth issue of *SoJourn*. Since our inaugural issue in spring 2016, we have published 62 articles on a wide range of South Jersey topics, along with 4 reviews of local museums or historical sites, and, in this issue, our first book review. We are hoping to keep this cooperative project underway for many years to come.

Stockton students serve as initial editors and designers for each article. We believe that the quality of *SoJourn* demonstrates their good work. We have received encouraging responses from these students, many who are clearly enthralled by South Jersey history; some are equally enthusiastic about editing for effective word choice and correct comma placement.

We have built a student-staffed local history press under the direction of Stockton's South Jersey Culture & History Center. To maintain our momentum, we ask for your support. We require a steady flow of articles written by the people who know our history best—you!

Below we review a selection of articles published in earlier issues of *SoJourn*. Can you or someone you know help us to write more?

"Mary, Mary, Quite Contrary . . ." (*SoJourn* 1.1). Patricia A. Martinelli provides an introduction to one of Vineland's more famous citizens, Mary Elizabeth Tillotson: "A petite blonde who dared to do something almost unheard of at the time—she donned trousers every day and rallied her sisters everywhere to do the same."

"Immersion" (*SoJourn* 1.1). In 1968, the State of New Jersey established a program in which bureaucratic folks were sent into various New Jersey cities disguised as homeless persons. Ken Tompkins, a founding Dean at Stockton, describes his experience in the program along with a second dean and Stockton's first president. They joined the program to experience the daily routine of the less fortunate and, perhaps, to assess whether public institutions provided adequate aid to this vulnerable population.

"The Future of Transportation: The Bicycle Railway" (*SoJourn* 1.1). Nineteenth-century Smithville, Burlington County, was a hotbed of innovation. Dennis McDonald spins a tale of Arthur Ethelbert Hotchkiss' short-lived, bicycle railway, which ran 1.8 miles across the winding Rancocas Creek from Mount Holly to Smithville.

"South Jersey Fruit Picking Tickets" (*SoJourn* 1.2). Rich Watson details the widespread practice of paying seasonal agricultural pickers with tokens and tickets that signified the amount of fruit or vegetables an individual picked. Watson focuses on local cranberry and blueberry farms including Budd's Bogs, Evans and Wills, Joseph Wharton, and the Cutts brothers. This article chronicles a time when farming was the dominant activity in many parts of South Jersey.

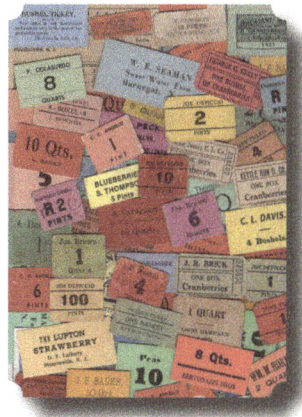

59

"Where Blackberries Grew: Margaret Mead in Hammonton" (*SoJourn* 1.2). Patricia Chapine and Mark Demitroff provide an introduction to Margaret Mead, the most renowned anthropologist of the twentieth century, explaining the importance of her early childhood spent in Hammonton. Home schooled, Mead learned the importance of practical skills. She became a student of local culture and of nature and applied her early lessons throughout her life and career.

"Alfred and Muriel: The Story of the J. A. Sweeton House in Cherry Hill, New Jersey" (*SoJourn* 1.2). This is the love story of J. A. Stanton and his wife Muriel, who completed a long-time dream of contacting Frank Lloyd Wright and convincing him to design a house for their property, a former peach orchard. This article, written by Brian Stolz as told by Jim Stanton, describes the lone Frank Lloyd Wright house built in South Jersey.

"Proving a Legend: A Submarine in the Rancocas Creek" (*SoJourn* 2.1). "Frank Astemborski remembered ghastly tales that the older boys told, scaring him into believing that dead men lay hidden inside a strange hull that they found partly submerged in the Riverside marsh." Here is a search for the truth behind the legends of a Civil War submarine whose hulk is reputed to be buried in a marsh along Rancocas Creek. Alice Smith proves that the submarine existed (two, in fact): Brutus de Villeroi designed and tested a prototype and a full-size submarine, the USS Alligator, in the early years of the Civil War. The Alligator sank in the Atlantic, but where is the prototype? Buried still along Rancocas Creek?

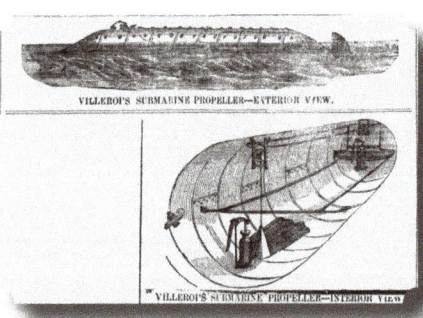

"Mapping the Mullica Valley: Natural History Landscapes" (*SoJourn* 2.1). This is the second of four articles written by, Kenneth W. Able, director of the Marine Field Station at Rutgers University, located on the Great Bay at the mouth of the Mullica River. Able explains the need to map both underwater and related terrestrial landscapes in order to study and evaluate change to those areas over time. The article is accompanied by a series of visually exciting aerial photographs and equally stunning images of the sea- and river-bed.

"Off Course in a Raging Sea: Captain William M. Phillips and the Plight of the Schooner Benjamin E. Valentine" (*SoJourn* 2.1). Based on documents held by Stockton University in the Estell-Bourgeois Collection, this article tells the story of one of Daniel Estell Jr.'s trading vessels whose home port was the Great Egg Harbor River. In January 1831, on a routine trip to deliver a cargo of corn meal and rye flour from Philadelphia to New York, the schooner sailed into a Nor'easter gale. The storm battered the ship for fourteen days, leaving it in perilous condition, when captain and crew found that they had been forced south to the eastern shore of Virginia. With ship and rigging completely clogged with ice, they ran to Norfolk as the nearest port for repairs. Delivering the now damaged cargo to New York would have to wait.

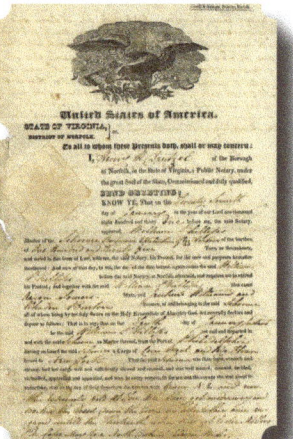

"Made in Nesco: The Inter-Generational Project of Place-Making" (*SoJourn* 2.2). Mary Jo Kietzman writes a moving history of her family in the Nesco

and Batsto area—the Wescoats, Southards and more. She describes the importance of place to forebears, to her mother, Catherine Alice (Midge) Walker Kietzman, and to herself. In doing so, she delves into truths that speak to us all. Where we come from does, indeed, matter and stories that we inherit or pass down about those places help us to understand the wider world.

"Calico or Dobbin's Bog" (*SoJourn* 2.2). In this, his third article written for *SoJourn*, Rich Watson turns his attention to locating the long vanished town of Calico in the heart of the Pine Barrens. Calico's history stretches back to the opening of the nineteenth century, when its cedar swamps, lowlands, and pine woods were associated with nearby Martha Furnace.  Watson traces the history of the tract through an early period of timber exploitation, followed by its use for cranberry agriculture and, later, blueberries. Through careful scholarship, paired with a deep knowledge of the Pines, Watson brings to life the rich cultural history of a once vibrant place, now largely forgotten.

 "Pocahontas on the Delaware: The Intersection of History and Legend in the Historiography of New Jersey" (*SoJourn* 2.2). John W. Lawrence traces the creation of the legend of Mahala, a so-named Native American woman whose interaction with early European explorers has grown into a story to rival that of Pocahontas. Factual details of the interaction between a Lenni-Lenape woman of the Sankitans band and Dutch patroon David Pieterszen de Vries are scarce, provided only by de Vries' brief journal entries. The woman is unnamed and her reasons for assisting the Europeans unclear. As Lawrence demonstrates, such lack of detail did not stop nineteenth-century historians from providing her with a name and full-blown relationship with de Vries. Here is a fascinating study of the intersection between South Jersey myth and history.

 "When Mad Anthony Came to South Jersey" (*SoJourn* 3.1). In this issue devoted to the Revolutionary War in South Jersey, Claude M. Epstein details the impact of military operations on the common citizen, with special attention to the foraging campaigns of American General Anthony Wayne and British Colonel Charles Mawhood. As contingents from either army approached, local farmers hid livestock in swamps, where the intruders lacked familiarity; nevertheless, horses, cattle, and other farm animals, along with large quantities of hay and foodstuffs, were confiscated or destroyed. With detail and empathy, Epstein describes the tragedies of war when South Jersey was a war zone.

"Knight at Egg Harbor" and "The Lord's Orders" (*SoJourn* 3.1). J. Anthony Harness has written two articles: the first describes a preliminary British naval raid in June 1777 on Egg Harbor Inlet at the mouth of the Mullica River; the second details the much more destructive Battle of Chestnut Neck during October 1778. The significance of South Jersey privateers operating from 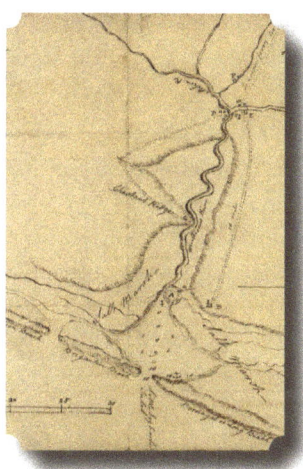 the Mullica is clear given the vigorous response by the British navy.

 "Research into the Battle of Gloucester" (*SoJourn* 3.1). Here is an outstanding introduction to South Jersey's significance to American military planning in Pennsylvania and New Jersey during the crucial period of late 1777. The military decisions of Washington, La Fayette, Nathanael Greene, Cornwallis and others are thoroughly discussed.

SoJourn

SoJourn 1.1 Spring 2016

"Nash's Cabin (Buck Run)" by Richard Watson, 7

"The Future of Transportation: The Bicycle Railway" by Dennis McDonald, 17

"Mary, Mary, Quite Contrary . . ." by Patricia A. Martinelli, 27

"Bipolar State: A Survey and Analysis of South Jersey's Geographical and Cultural Borders" by Robert Lowe Barnett and Steve Chernoski, 33

"Immersion" by Kenneth Tompkins, 49

"Shinplasters: Economic Remnants of New Jersey's Glass Industry" by Todd R. Sciore, 55

"The Burlington Town Plan: From Medieval to Modern" by Robert P. Thompson, 63

"Nature, Naturalists, and South Jersey" by Claude M. Epstein, 75

"Mary Ann and the Cranberry Farm, a Transformative Experience" by Alexis Demitroff, 89

SoJourn 1.2 Winter 2016/17

"Kate Aylesford: Modernity and Place in New Jersey's Pine Barrens" by Matthew G. Hatvany, 7

"Alfred and Muriel: The Story of the J. A. Sweeton House in Cherry Hill, New Jersey" by Brian Stolz as told by Jim Stanton, 19

"School Segregation in the Post-Civil War Era: Burlington County, New Jersey, 1865–1915" by Zachary T. Baer, 25

"Where Blackberries Grew: Margaret Mead in Hammonton" by Patricia Chappine and Mark Demitroff, 37

"A Day on the Bay with Waterman Phil Andersen" by Susan Allen, 45

"South Jersey Fruit Picking Tickets" by Richard Watson, 50

"From Butcher Knife to Scalpel: Four Generations of South Jersey Physicians" by Lisa E. Cox, Edward Hutton and Ruth Hutton-Williams, 63

"Manufacturing from Menhaden: A History in the Mullica Valley" by Kenneth W. Able, 75

"Carabajal, The Jew: A Legend of Monterey, Mexico" by Charles K. Landis, 83

"Reimagining a Remnant of the Past at Stockton" by James Pullaro and Paul W. Schopp, 100

SoJourn 2.1 Summer 2017

"The First African American Excursion to Atlantic City" by Paul W. Schopp, 7

"Proving a Legend: A Submarine in the Rancocas Creek" by Alice Smith, 15

"Brevet Brigadier General Elias Wright: Surveyor Extraordinaire" by Elizabeth G. Carpenter, 23

"Mapping the Mullica Valley: Natural History Landscapes" by Kenneth W. Able, 33

"Off Course in a Raging Sea: Captain William M. Phillips and the Plight of the Schooner Benjamin E. Valentine" by Paul W. Schopp with Anthony Ficcaglia, 45

"Haul Away, Boys!" 53

"Jerseyisms" by Francis E. Lee, 59

"The Rebirth of Buzby's Chatsworth General Store" by R. Marilyn Schmidt, 68

"The Publications of R. Marilyn Schmidt," 78

"The Endicott-Reardon Family Museum" by Rebecca Muller, 81

"Anecdotes and Memoirs of William Boen," 85

"The Coia Map Project" by James Pullaro and Paul W. Schopp, 94

SoJourn 2.2 Winter 2017/18

"Made in Nesco: The Inter-Generational Project of Place-Making" by Mary Jo Kietzman, 7

"Le Balloonist" by Hal Taylor, 23

"Elizabeth C. White's Garden" by Albertine Senske, 28

"Pocahontas on the Delaware: The Intersection of History and Legend in the Historiography of New Jersey" by John W. Lawrence, 39

"Calico or Dobbin's Bog" by Rich Watson, 53

"Plagues and Public Policy: How South Jersey Cleaned Up Its Act" by Claude Epstein, 69

"Stockton University Welcomes Heather Perez: Special Collections Librarian and Archivist" by Amy Krieger, 83

"Ghost Forests in the Mullica Valley: Indicators of Sea-Level Rise" by Kenneth W. Able, Jennifer Walker, and Benjamin P. Horton, 87

"A February Freshet & Breach in the Bank" by Dallas Lore Sharp, 97

SoJourn 3.1 Summer 2018

"Battle of Turtle Gut Inlet" by Zachary T. Baer and Paul W. Schopp, 7

"The Battle of Iron Works Hill" by Salvatore D. Gabriele, 17

"Knight at Egg Harbor" by J. Anthony Harness, 31

"Forgotten Victories" by Jeffery M. Dorwart, 41

"Research into the Battle of Gloucester" by Garry Wheeler Stone, Paul W. Schopp, and Jason R. Wickertsty, 55

"The Battle of the Kegs" by Francis Hopkinson, 74

"Should New Jersey Be Considered the Crossroads of the American Revolution?" by Zachary T. Baer, 77

"When Mad Anthony Came to South Jersey" by Claude M. Epstein, 81

"The Lord's Orders" by J. Anthony Harness, 95

"Born a Peacemaker, Became a Patriot: 1st Lieutenant Jeremiah Leeds" by Norman Reeves Goos, 107

"Notice is Hereby Given: Extracts from Colonial Newspapers," 120

"South Jersey's Revolutionary Battles, Skirmishes, and Future Research," 127

"Cedar Bridge Tavern," 137

"The Atlantic County Veterans Museum," by Jackson Glassey, 141

Back issues of *SoJourn* are available from the SJCHC, Second Time Books in Mount Laurel, and Amazon.com.

The Newton Union Burial Ground:
The Site of Camden County's Origin and The Resting Place of Its Early Pioneers

Robert Shinn, Andrew Levecchia, and Sandra White Grear

In 1681 five members of the Religious Society of Friends chartered a 46-foot pink—a type of ship—to transport 21 emigrants from Ireland to Salem, West New Jersey. Thomas Sharp, one of the five Friends, wrote the following account of the adventure in 1728:

> Let it be remembered yt[1] upon ye nineteenth day of September, in ye year of our Lord one thousand six hundred and eighty-one, Mark Newby, William Bates, Thomas Thackara, George Goldsmith and Thomas Sharp, set saile from ye Harbor belonging to ye city of Dublin, in ye Kingdom of Ireland, in a pink called 'Ye owners adventure,' whereof Thomas Lurtin, of London, was commander, and being taken sick in ye city, his mate, John Dagger, officiated in his place; in order to transport us, and yt we might settle ourselves in West Jersey, in America. And by ye good providence of God we arrived in ye Capes of Delaware ye eighteenth day of November following, and so up ye bay until we came to Elsinburg, and were landed with our goods and families at Salem, where we abode ye winter. But it being very favourable weather and purchasing a boat amongst us, we had an opportunity to make search up and down in yt which was called ye Third tenth, which had been reserved for ye proprietors dwelling in Ireland, where we might find a place suitable for so many of us to settle down together, being in these early times somewhat doubtful of ye Indians, and at last pitched down by yt which is now called Newton creek, as ye most invitingist place to settle down by, and then we went to Burlington, and made application to ye commissioners yt we might have warrants directed to Daniel Leeds, ye Surveyor General, to survey unto every of us, so much land as by ye constitution at yt time was allotted for a settlement being five hundred acres, or yt we had a right to, for a taking up it under, which accordingly we obtained.[2]

Figure 1. A Pink. This type of craft brought the first pioneers here. Drawing from Raymond Mitchell Bancroft, *Collingswood Story* (Collingswood, NJ, Borough of Collingswood, 1965).

A year later, in 1729, the author's friends and neighbors paid him their last respects. Thomas Sharp was the last of the five Friends who "departed this life, and was, no doubt, buried in the old Newton grave yard."[3] Other English Friends and their families closely followed the five into the Third Tenth and eventually their remains joined Sharp's in the Newton Burial Ground.[4] Others, including William Cooper, William Roydon, and Samuel Norris, had acquired land in the Tenth before the five Friends had arrived.[5]

The Third Tenth extended along the Delaware River between the Big Timber and Pennsauken creek.[6] The Third Tenth[7] settlers were on the vanguard of a huge English Friends migration to the Delaware Valley that began in Salem in 1675 and continued in Burlington during 1677. The year after the five friends arrived, 23 ships sailed up the Delaware carrying an aggregate of about 2000 Friends bound primarily for Pennsylvania.[8] Thousands of Friends followed and dominated the culture and government of Pennsylvania and West New Jersey up to the middle of the eighteenth century.

Why They Emigrated

Religious persecution provided a powerful impetus for the first migration of the Friends to these two mid-Atlantic colonies.[9] A fifth of West New Jersey Friends, and half of those who migrated to Pennsylvania, suffered fines and imprisonment.[10] Government officials continually persecuted Friends for opposing tithes to the Church of England.[11] From 1685 to 1750, magistrates deprived Friends of £92,745 and imprisoned 91 adherents.[12] Later, after persecutions subsided following Parliament's passage of the Acts of Toleration in 1689, it would appear that economic restrictions had greater influence upon migration.[13]

Most of the Friends emigrating from Ireland were of English birth,[14] but departed their native land to escape persecution.[15] In Ireland, however, the irritations and annoyances eventually proved to be just as harsh. The future West New Jersey proprietors "were charged with countless transgressions and misdemeanors: refusal to attend the service of the national church, refusal to pay tithes, refusal to contribute to the building and to the repair of churches, refusal to close their shops on Christian holidays, refusal to remove their hats in church or in the presence of officials, refusal to defray charges for the support of the militia, refusal to take oaths, and refusal to pay fines."[16]

But Where Could They Go?

Prior to 1677, Friends could not escape persecution by emigrating to North America. In 1660, one catalogue of maltreatment of New England Friends listed 64 imprisoned; two lashed 139 times "like into a jelly;" another branded with the letter "H" for heretic, after being whipped with 39 stripes; and three executed.[17] Friends even faced hostility in New Amsterdam, which generally tolerated a variety of religious sects. Dutch authorities fined, jailed, and banished Friends arriving in Long Island in 1657. Like Puritan New Englanders, the Dutch were outraged by proselytizing women Friends. Friends faced similar persecution in Virginia and, to a lesser degree, in Maryland.

The door to establishing a Religious Society of Friends colony in North America cracked opened in 1673, after Dutch warships returned to the Delaware River to recapture New Amstel and land previously lost to the British in 1664.[18] This precipitated Sir John Berkeley, a bankrupt member of King Charles II Privy Council, to sell his moiety

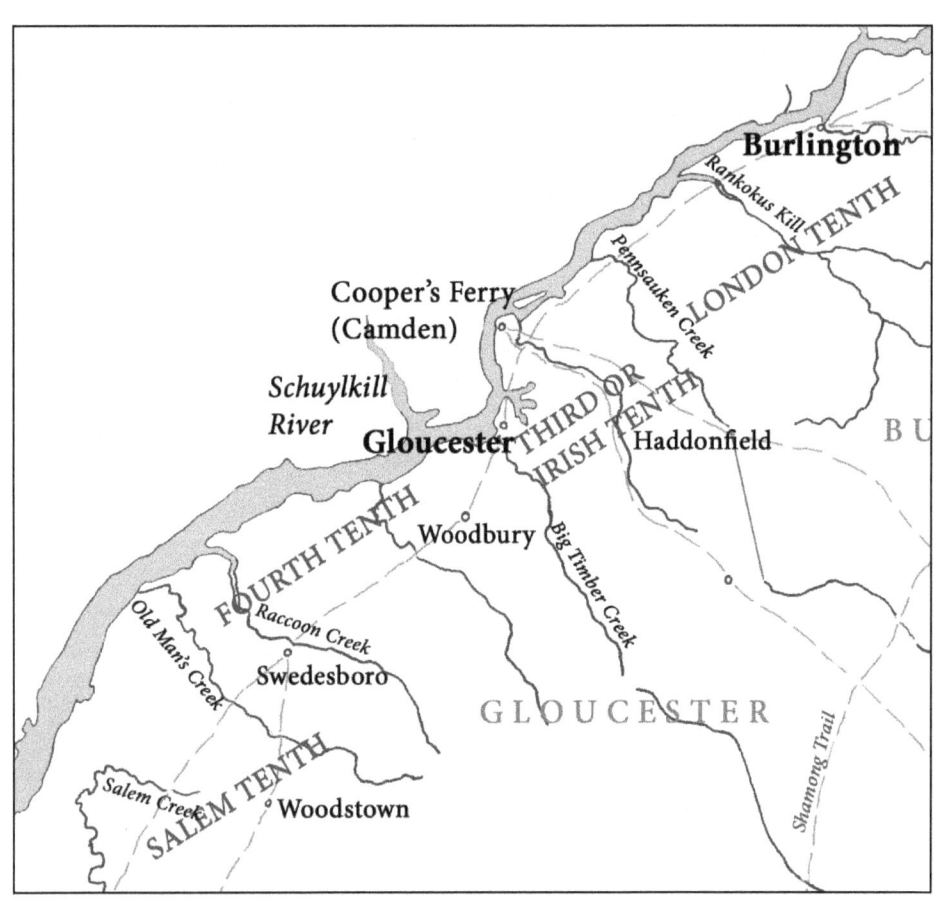

Figure 2. Map of 1682 West New Jersey showing the Third or Irish Tenth, from *Goodspeed Histories* blog, November 11, 2009, https://goodspeedhistories.com/west-new-jersey-1682/.

The Newton Union Burial Ground

Figure 3. Quaker Mary Dyer being led to the gallows in Boston, 1660. Painting by Howard Pyle c. 1905, published in *McClure's*, 1907. From the collection of the Newport Historical Society. Courtesy of Wikimedia.

or half-interest in New Jersey.[19] The door swung wide open on March 18, 1674, when London brewer Edward Byllynge, an early and prominent member of the Society of Friends,[20] purchased that interest from his crony Berkeley for £1,000.[21] Berkeley had suggested that Byllynge purchase half of New Jersey as a way for Byllynge to recoup his shattered fortunes. Because Byllynge was also bankrupt, he arranged for John Fenwick to purchase Berkeley's interest "in trust" for him so that his name did not appear in the conveyance.[22] Both Fenwick and Byllynge had served under Cromwell before later joining the Society of Friends.[23] Fenwick reportedly obtained the deeds by fraud and refused to give them over until Byllynge agreed to grant Fenwick one full tenth.[24] London Friends pressured both parties to allow William Penn to arbitrate the matter, rather than go to court. Byllynge asked Penn, together with Friends Gawen Laurie and Nicholas Lucas, to manage a trust on his behalf. Penn arranged to subdivide West Jersey from East Jersey and to form a joint stock company as a means of raising capital with 100 shares valued at £350 each. Thus, what Fenwick and Byllynge had purchased for £1000, would be worth £35,000 with the sale of all shares. One share would obtain 1/100 of West New Jersey as equity.[25]

The planting of Friends colonies then proceeded, following the issuance of the West Jersey Concessions and Agreements of March 3, 1677. Written by Edward Byllynge and William Penn,[26] the Concessions and Agreements were a great inducement to emigrate to West New Jersey. They promised religious freedom, equitable taxation, and representative government. These provisions were remarkable in light of the increasing persecution of Friends in England.[27] The Concessions were the most liberal and comprehensive set of individual liberties set forth in the Americas. The American Bill of Rights included many of its provisions a century later, and New Jersey was the first state to ratify the Bill of Rights. One month after the Concessions were issued, five Dublin tradesmen purchased a propriety[28] in West Jersey.[29] Four of them (Robert Turner, Robert Zane, Thomas Thackara, and William Bates) intended to settle there.[30]

Where They Went

During the mild winter following their arrival, the five emigrants joined their advanced scout, Robert Zane,[31] and purchased a boat to "find a place suitable for so many of us to settle." They went to Burlington to obtain a survey warrant and, after "some considerable search to and fro," they found "Ye most invitingist place" along the north shore of Newton Creek. They could not find any agricultural land available along the Delaware River across from the future site of Philadelphia. William Cooper,[32] who originally settled in Burlington, and other West Jersey Friends, may have heard about plans for Philadelphia[33] and acquired those arable lands before the six men launched their search.[34] In spring 1682, the emigrants surveyed 100 acres of meadow at the mouth of Little Newton creek, later known as Kaighn's Run or Line Ditch, and 1600 acres on the Newton Creek, an area now known as the West Collingswood Extension section of Haddon Township.[35]

William Bates took up his "twentieth share" of land on the south side of Newton Creek,[36] while the others settled on one tract together, comprising 1750 acres. They built cabins proximate to each other, forming a small village, which they called Newton."[37] After some time, the settlers "finding some inconveniency in having our land in common together" and finding "the Indians in the region peaceable," they agreed to divide the land as shown in Figure 5, build houses on their own land, and abandon the original village.[38]

Newton Meeting Burial Ground and Meeting House

The first six people and their families established a Friends Meeting at Mark Newbie's house and laid out a burial ground on two acres donated by Thomas Thackara.[39] The burial ground was one of the first in West New Jersey. In 1684, they built a log meetinghouse that may have resembled the log building in Figure 6.

William Bates developed the plans and served as the primary builder. Figure 7 locates the "Quaker Burial Ground" (LOT A) and where the "Meeting House Stood" (LOT B).[40]

Note the location of two large Buttonwood trees, which some have suggested were planted to shade the meeting house, and the 45' x 60' dotted line square area marked off across Lynne Avenue between Eldredge and Elm with the names "Jos. Sloan to Jas. Sloan" in the middle connected by an arrow to text indicating the location of a deed (Book W-Folio 585 Oct 16, 1810) "Whereon The Old Meeting House Stands." Figure 7 indicates the "Probable Original Landing Wharf" location. The small "no-man's land" parcel between the two burial grounds shown was once a lane that led from the meeting house to a landing wharf. Faint remains of the wharf were visible in 1939. It was about 20 feet wide and extended out about 30 feet. An excavated channel permitted access at low tides.[41]

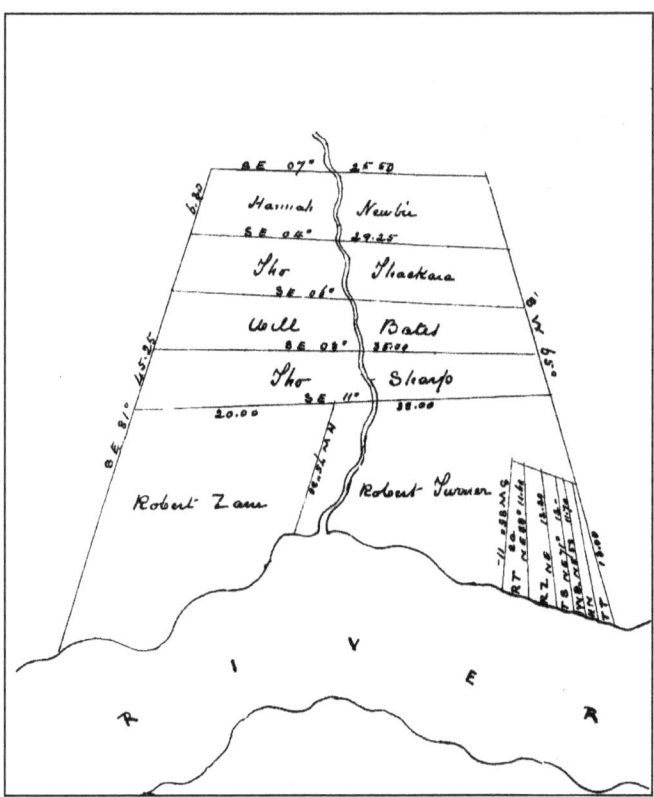

Figure 4. Map of "The Meadow belongs to the Town of Newton" from John Clement, *Sketches of the First Emigrant Settlers Newton Township Old Gloucester County, West Jersey* (Camden, NJ: Sinnickson Chew, 1877), end sheet.

Figure 5. "... Thomas Sharp's Map A.D. 1700, of lands lying between the South Branch of Newton Creek and Cooper's Creeks, mostly included in the original bounds of Newton Township, Gloucester County ..." from John Clement, *Sketches of the First Emigrant Settlers Newton Township Old Gloucester County, West Jersey* (Camden, NJ: Sinnickson Chew, 1877), end sheet.

The Newton Union Burial Ground

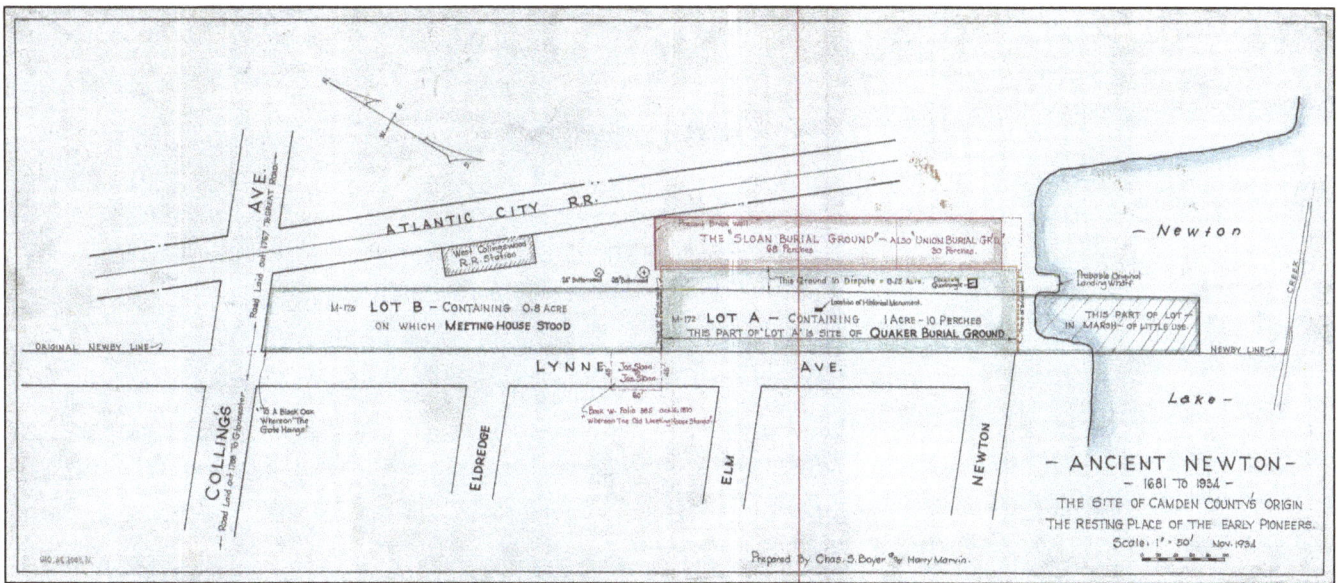

Figure 6. Example of a log Friends' Meeting House. Roaring Creek Friends Meeting House, Quaker Meeting Road, Numidia, Columbia County, Pennsylvania. Courtesy of the Library of Congress, HABS PA 6691-32 (CT).

Figure 7. "Ancient Newton, 1681 to 1934, The Site of Camden County's Origin; The Resting Place of the Early Pioneers," Charles S. Boyer and Harry Marvin, manuscript map (Camden, NJ: Camden County Historical Society, November 1934).

The Newton Meeting House was the first in Camden (and Old Gloucester) County and the third in West New Jersey.[42] A board of trustees supervised the Newton Meeting and burial ground. Thomas Thackara, William Cooper, and William Albertson served as the first trustees. In 1708, the trustees included William Albertson, Thomas Sharp, John Kaighn, William and Joseph Cooper, Benjamin Thackara, and John Kay.

Newton Meeting removed to Haddonfield circa 1715.[43] The Haddonfield Friends build a log meeting house on land John Haddon donated where the Haddonfield Fire House stands today. They held their first Meeting for Worship in the Haddonfield Meeting House on December 12, 1721.[44] Friends continued using the Newton Meeting Burial Ground after the meeting's relocation. The Newton Meeting Burial Ground was declared "full prior to 1842."[45] Local residents continued to occupy the old Newton Meeting House for local government functions and as the township's first school until a fire swept through the old log structure.[46]

WHO LIES IN REPOSE AT NEWTON?

Newton Burial Ground holds the remains of most of Old Gloucester County's (which includes current day Camden County) founders, first families, and immediate descendants.[47] These include all descendants who died prior to the Haddonfield Monthly Meeting opening its own graveyard in 1720 and those not buried in private plots.[48] Families later buried descendant Friends in the New Newton Friends Meeting burial ground after it opened in Camden in 1801.[49] Some of the more prominent old Newton Meeting families[50] interred in the Newton Burial Ground include:

William Cooper, a blacksmith from Coleshill, Amersham, Hertfordshire, England, and the first English Friend to settle in the Third Tenth. Cooper and his family arrived in Burlington first, where he located 50 acres in the fall of 1680. Shortly thereafter, Cooper located and took up, as part of his proprietorship, a 300-acre plantation he called Pyne Poynt, situated proximate to the confluence of the Delaware River and Deer Creek (now the Cooper River). Cooper held worship meetings in his house for Pennsylvania and West Jersey Friends in 1682. Cooper served as an advisor to William Penn and attended his famous treaty meeting with the Lenapes at Shackamaxon in 1683. Cooper later acquired the rights to operate a ferry and adjacent lands from William Roydon, who had his land surveyed before Cooper. Starting with this acquired license, the Cooper family operated a ferry service between Coopers Ferry (now Camden) and Philadelphia for 150 years. The Third Tenth elected Cooper as their Assemblyman in 1682, 1683, and 1685. Cooper served as Commissioner for Dividing and Regulating Lands in the Province of West New Jersey. Cooper provided financial and political support to the local "right of government" claims of Governor Samuel Jennings and Thomas Budd against the counter claims of Edward Byllynge. Cooper defended the Friends orthodoxy against the schism initiated by George Keith and signed statements against Keith on behalf of the Newton and the Philadelphia Yearly Meetings to the London Yearly Meeting. He was elected Judge of the Gloucester County Common Pleas Court in 1696. He accumulated sufficient land and wealth to enable his children and grandchildren to assume business and government leadership positions in West New Jersey. Upon his death in 1710, Cooper's remains were carried through the woods from his home at Coopertown (now part of Cherry Hill) to the Newton Burial Ground.[51]

Thomas Sharp, Irish "woolstead comber." Sharp had a better education than most of his contemporaries, and, although he was a young man when he arrived at Newton Colony, his sea voyage companions had confidence in him. Sharp had studied law. He was a nephew of Anthony Sharp, a wealthy merchant of Dublin, who purchased several propriety shares, part of which he gave to Thomas, who also acted as his agent in the sale of the remaining land rights. The Newton Colony and West New Jersey Province entrusted Sharp with a variety of civic posts over his lifetime: area constable (sheriff); Newton Township clerk; first Gloucester County clerk and surveyor; highway commissioner; member of the Assembly; urban planner of the city of Gloucester; map maker;[52] judge; trustee of the Newton Meeting; and county freeholder. Sharp helped build the first Newton Meeting House and aided in establishing the Haddonfield Meeting House. He selected its site, surveyed its lot, and prepared its deed. Sharp wrote the early history of Newton Township and Gloucester County[53] and prepared many local survey maps.

Thomas Thackara, a native of Yorkshire, England, and a "stuff weaver" from Dublin. Thackara was a man of some estate and acquainted with fellow Friend and linen merchant Robert Turner. Thackara donated two acres of his land for the Newton Burial Ground and Meeting House. Thackara held a variety of civic posts in Newton: member of the first Assembly that framed and adopted laws for the province, judge for the Irish Tenth, member of the Council of Proprietors in 1688, and land commissioner for the province. Thackara signed the address of the Newton meeting to the yearly meeting of London, protesting against the conduct of George Keith, in his differences with the Society of Friends.

John Kaighn, a native of the Isle of Man and a carpenter. Kaighn first emigrated to Byberry, Pennsylvania, circa 1690, before marrying the daughter of William Albertson of Newton. Kaighn purchased 450 acres from Robert Turner fronting on the Delaware River and extending from today's Line Street to Little Newton Creek.[54] Kaighn served in a variety of public and Friends functions: Gloucester County judge, Gloucester County Assembly representative, and trustee of the Newton monthly meeting. John Kaighn's "remains doubtless lie buried within the walls that now surround part of the first estate dedicated to such purposes in this region of the country."[55]

Mark Newbie, a tallow chandler in London before moving to Dublin in 1681 to escape religious persecution. Newbie's move to Dublin was temporary —accomplished "with a view to settling in America and making it his permanent home."[56] Newbie aided in selecting the site for the Newton Colony and hosted its first Friends meetings in his home, the fourth in West New Jersey. He held several important public offices: Assembly member, Governor's Council member, Commissioner for the division of land in the West Jersey Province, and Ways and Means Committee member to raise money for the government's use. Newbie served with William Cooper on a committee to address the "right of government issue," which the early settlers understood the Concessions and Agreements had conveyed, but which Edward Byllynge later denied. Newbie was the founder of the first bank in New Jersey, providing hard money in the form of "Patrick Halfpence," copper tokens struck in Ireland after the massacre of Roman Catholics in 1641.[57] Because West New Jersey had a shortage of small coins, the Assembly passed the following in May 1682: "For the convenient Payment of small sums, be it enacted that Mark Newbie's half pence, from and after the Eighteenth instant, pass for halfpence current pay of the province...." The Assembly required Newbie to put up, as security to the Speaker of the Assembly, a tract of 300 acres. Newbie died in 1683, the first of the "Irish five" to pass away. He was among the first, if not the first, to be buried in the Newton Burial Ground.[58]

Friends Burial Grounds—Plain and Simple

Between 1620 and 1660, wooden markers constructed like a section of fence with two posts anchored in the ground and a plank fitted between them for the deceased's name served to identify common English graves.[50] Only members of the nobility and gentry had elaborate headstones marking their graves. Friends brought the tradition of no headstones to West New Jersey and strongly discouraged or banned stone markers. A survey of the Shrewsbury Friends Burial Ground in 1886 recorded four remaining "wooden head pieces" among 133 markers.[60] Even today, Friends maintain simple, unadorned burial grounds.[61]

Virtually all of the original Newton settlers' graves and their family members in the Friends' section of the Newton Union Burial Ground did not feature tombstones. The Disciplines of Philadelphia Yearly Meeting specifically forbade grave markers of any kind until the last quarter of the nineteenth century. They viewed such markers as "Marks of Superfluity and excess" and "inconsistent with the plainness of our Principles and Practice."[62] Friends believed that even in death they should bear testimony against practices that promote human vanity. Early colonial Friends' burial grounds in North American could be identified as simple unbroken fields of unmarked graves. Depending on the location, they could either have a physical perimeter, usually a stone wall, or remain open. Even after the Friends began using marble grave markers, they were largely devoid of ornamentation from the early eighteenth century well into the nineteenth.[63]

This tradition changed in the mid-nineteenth century, when the Society of Friends' discipline evolved to generally accept small, simple tombstones.[64] Part of the Newton Union Burial Ground can be identified for having simple stones, though many dates are unreadable. Friends placed strict limits on the stone's dimensions and permitted no epitaphs, decorations, or additions: "... in each particular burial ground, such uniformity

Figure 8. Patrick Halfpence (1670–75). St. Patrick Farthing, Breen-208, VF30, authorized New Jersey coinage. Copper token brought from Ireland by Mark Newbie. Image courtesy of Heritage Auctions, http://www.ha.com.

is preserved in respect to the materials, size, form and wording of the stones, as well as in the mode of placing them, as may effectually guard against any distinction being made in that place between the rich and the poor."[65]

The evolution towards marked graves was controversial. Samuel Nicholson, a conservative nineteenth-century Friend, was not able to accept headstones on grave sites. Nicholson lived next to the Haddonfield Friends Burial Ground.[66] "The story is told that Samuel Nicholson, who died in 1877, disapproved of gravestones and he would push them below ground level. Others would later come along and resurrect the grave-markers."[67] Friends also disapproved of elaborate funeral processions. The coffin was placed in the ground prior to holding a meeting. Sometimes a meeting would proceed and then the coffin carried to the graveside. Friends believed seeing the corpse in the meeting and then carrying the coffin to the burial ground and watching the interment was useful for "the propagation of truth."[68]

But on at least one occasion in July 1703, Newton's dependence on rivers for transportation and widespread public esteem for the deceased combined to create an elegant, if simple, funeral procession. Funeral processions, like most travel, occurred using riverine transportation. One such procession, following multiple deaths from a lightning strike, was so noteworthy that William Penn received a letter from James Logan, his colonial secretary, stating that[69] "on the 24th between 9 and 10 at night, Esther Spicer, widow, as she was undressing in bed in her own house was struck dead with two of her servants, three more escaping."[70] Two days later, Friends moved the bodies to the Newton Burial Ground accompanied by 30 boats and 400 people:

> The funeral was by night, the family and friends going in boats down Coopers creek to the river Delaware, and down the river to Newton creek, and thence to Newton graveyard. Each boat being provided with torches the scene upon the water must have been picturesque indeed. To the colonists, it was a sad spectacle when they saw one so much esteemed among them being borne to her last resting place. To the Indians it was a grand and impressive sight. Arasapha, the king, and others of his people, attended the

Figure 9. A charcoal sketch which attempts to depict a scene from "Esther Spicer's funeral procession," Jack H. Fichter, *A History of Pennsauken Township*, sketch by Edmund J. Halber (Pennsauken, NJ: Pennsauken Historical Society, 1966).

solemn procession in their canoes, thus showing respect for one, the cause of whose death struck them with awe and reverence. The deep, dark forest that stood close down to the shores of the stream almost rejected the light as it came from the burning brands of pine carried in the boats, and as they passed under the thick foliage a shadow was scarcely reflected from the water.[71]

Sloan Burial Ground Scandal

Theological schisms occurred among the Society of Friends in the early 1700s, during the American Revolution, and in the late 1820s, when Elias Hicks and his theology divided the brethren.[72,73] Orthodox Friends disowned or "read out of meetings" those who violated Friends' discipline and core teachings, including violating their Peace Testimony through support or participation in the American Revolution. Newton Meeting prohibited the burial of any Friends who had been "read out of meeting" in the Newton Burial Ground.

James Sloan founded the Sloan or Union Burying Ground on one acre he purchased from James Thackara adjacent to the old Newton Burying Ground due to a dispute with the Society of Friends. According to local historian Charles S. Boyer,

> The real cause of this dispute has always been a mystery, the older accounts stating that it was over the boundary lines of the old Newton Burying Ground and the adjoining lands of James and Joseph Sloan. Investigations which have been made lately, however, would indicate that this dispute had a much deeper significance. The boundary dispute over a strip of land of less than a quarter of an acre would scarcely involve parties in a feud that lasted for over ten years and amounted almost to a scandal among Quakers. Probably the real animus which led to the founding of the Sloan Burying Ground was that none but Quakers could be buried in the old grounds, or the edict that no monuments should be erected to mark the last resting place of the departed. Some of James Sloan's children had married "out of meeting," and either or both of these reasons can be read into the tablet[74] which James Sloan placed on the brick wall around the grounds, which read as follows:

> Here is no distinction. Rich and Poor meet together the Lord is maker of them all Founded by James Sloan 1790.[75]

Newton Meeting disowned James Sloan because he "hath for some time past so far given way to a separating spirit as to appoint meetings under a profession of worship in which meeting he has undertaken to appear as a minister; which conduct being a manifest deviation from our disciplines a disownment was entirely proper and necessary."[76]

Sloan divided his burial ground into sixty lots which he sold to Newton Colony descendants.[77] The Sloan cemetery also contains a designated "poor row" of unmarked graves.

A past president of the Newton Union School Society said Sloan established his separate burial ground because Friends discriminated against young men from the Newton Meeting who fought in the American Revolution"[78] Sloan was particularly interested in providing burial grounds for James Sloan, who had been in the militia, for his daughter and her husband, who had also been in the militia, and for his children who married "out of meeting."[79] There are 22 veterans of the Ameri-

Table 1. Veterans of the American Revolution and the War of 1812 buried in the Sloan Burying Ground	
Ephraim Albertson, Pvt. GCM* 1742–Unknown	John T. Dill, Pvt. GCM 1762–1845
Isaac Albertson, Lt. GCM 1763–1823	Jacob Evaul, Pvt. (Capt.?) Mass Militia 1764–1838
Jacob Albertson, Sr., Pvt. 1714–1761	Joseph Githens, Pvt. GCM–Unknown
Jacob Albertson, Jr., Pvt./Ensign 1730–1806	David Henry, Pvt. 16 Pa Inf, War 1812 1799–1826
Josiah Albertson, Lt., GCM 1737–Unknown	Robert Henry, Pvt. GCM 1754–1825
Joseph Albertson, Pvt. GCM 1750–1831	John Heritage, Pvt./Sgt GCM 1740–1817
Joseph Branson	William Knight, Pvt. GCM 1750–1797
George Budd, Pvt. GCM 1737–1815	James Sloan, Pvt. GCM 1740–1782
Joseph Zane Collings, Pvt. GCM 1763–1818	John Thackara, Am. Rev. Unknown–1827
Edward Zane Collings, Pvt. GCM 1763–1820	William (Joseph?) Wolohorn, 5th Class, NJ Militia, Unknown
James Coulter, Pvt. GCM 1742–1811	William Wright, Pvt, GCM 1751–1811
* Note: GCM = Gloucester Co. Militia, Revolutionary War	

can Revolution and two from the War of 1812 buried in Sloan's Burial Ground. Most Revolutionary War veterans were members of the Gloucester County Militia. The Sloan's Burial Ground holds the largest number of American Revolutionary War veteran graves in southern New Jersey. Table 1 lists their names, ranks, birth and death years.[80]

This list indicates that at least two officers and fifteen privates who served in the Gloucester County Militia during the American Revolution are buried in the Sloan Section. At one time, some of these men were under the command of captains John Stokes, John Wood, William Harrison, or Jacob Browning. There are at least seven additional veterans not in Table 1 who may be buried in the Sloan Section, but whose burials have not yet been confirmed.[81] Another veteran of the War of 1812, who served in the "Camden Blues" under the command of Captain Newton and is buried in the Sloan section, is James Vennell, who literally died on the job. As sexton of the Newton Burial Ground, while attending upon a funeral, and immediately after lowering the coffin into the grave, the 79 year old Vennell fell back and expired.[82] A Works Progress Administration October 1937 Survey of the location and contents of the Sloan Burial Ground[83] identified the burial locations of some of the veterans of the American Revolution.[84]

In 1811, Joseph Sloan, son of James, abandoned his claim of his deed to the Trustees of the Haddonfield Meeting. The land so deeded extended to the old graveyard within the brick wall and some adjoining property. The whole burial ground with both the Newton Burial Ground and Sloan Burial Ground has since become known as the Newton Union Burial Ground.[85] According to the legible headstones, the last three people buried in the Sloan section are Mary P. Powell (1808–1909), Joseph Stokes (1844–1909), and Anna M. Collings (1848–1931).

Meetinghouse School Moves to Champion School

The Newton Meeting House burned down on December 22, 1817. Local residents made no effort to rebuild it.[86] Instead, those in the area formed the Newton Union School Society and sold stock at five dollars a share to raise funds for a new school, but needed a new location as the original building was on land that Sloan had acquired. The residents approached the Haddonfield Monthly Meeting to purchase a piece of the old, unused burial ground. In June 1821, the Haddonfield Monthly agreed to sell for $75. Three years after building the school, the school society realized they never remitted or received a deed. Samuel C. Champion paid the $75 and had the land deeded in his name and his wife, Elizabeth Zane-Champion's[87] name, along with a stipulation that the property would remain in use as a schoolhouse for educational purposes. In 1838, the school society purchased the property from Champions for $110. The Champion School was named the first free school in Old Gloucester County. The Champion School closed in 1907 when the Collingswood Borough School Board completed the Thomas Sharp School in West Collingswood. The Champion School is listed in the New Jersey and National Registers of Historic Places during 1988.[88]

Burial Ground Status in the Nineteenth and Twentieth Centuries

The 1850 *Plan of the Townships of Union and Newton*, a portion of which is reproduced as Figure 10, indicates that the Friends Graveyard (located between Newton Creek Main Branch and Race Course Road and between Mount Ephraim Road and White Horse Road) remained in a rural area halfway through the nineteenth century, with large tracts of farmland belonging to the Champions, E. Smith, and J. Campbell surrounding the buring place.

In 1886, historian George R. Prowell described the burial ground as enclosed "by a brick wall, and is overgrown by low trees and vines."[89] In 1891, the Atlantic City Railroad Company,[90] the Collingswood Land Company, and Champion Land Company purchased lands adjacent to the Newton Burial Ground for $800, predicated on the land remaining unbuilt upon and serving as a free and open public park surrounding the hallowed ground.

A 1909 photo in Figure 11 shows the brick wall along the northern end of the Newton Union Burial Ground extant and that most headstones within view south of the wall remained standing, intact, and in good condition. Removal of the brick wall occurred in the 1920s.[91]

Efforts to preserve the burial ground began in 1927, when the Haddonfield Friends Committee in charge of Newton Union Burial Ground started to raise a Trust Fund "to restore the grounds and make them a thing of beauty."[92] In 1931, however, Haddonfield Meeting members removed all headstones in the Friends' section and leveled the ground.[93] Descendants of South Jersey's settlers called the move a "historical outrage" and formed an organization to perpetuate the landmark as a historic shrine.[94] The Haddonfield Friends reported they could no longer properly maintain the burial ground due to a lack of funds. "You had no right to do that," Frank Stewart, President of the Gloucester County Historical

The Newton Union Burial Ground

Figure 10. Detail from the *Plan of the Townships of Union and Newton Newton, County of Camden* by James C. Sidney (Philadelphia, PA: Richard Clark, 1850) showing the location of the "Friends Grave Yard" and adjacent School House in Newton Township. The red circle identifies the location of the Friends Grave Yard and adjacent Champion School House in Newton Township.

Society, almost shrieked, "*this is the greatest historical outrage ever perpetrated in South Jersey, and Quaker though I am, I could go outside and fight anybody who opposes our plans*"(bold and italics added for emphasis).[95] After some agitation, the Friends "placed the Burial Ground in order" by returning the old broken headstones and embedding them in concrete (see Figure 13) in the wall of a memorial erected at the southeast end of the burial ground. (See Figure 14 for location.)

In 1931, the Camden County Historical Society erected a stone monument[96] in the middle of the northwest section of Newton Union Burial Ground Section near the intersection of Lynne and Elm Avenues with a bronze plaque (See Figure 14 for location) with the following inscription taken from John Clement's *First Emigrant Settlers in Newton Township*, first published in 1877:

OLD NEWTON FRIENDS
BURIAL GROUND

Near this site in 1681, Mark Newby, William Bates, Thomas Thackara, George Goldsmith, Thomas Sharp, Robert Zane, and others, immigrants from Ireland, who came here in quest of religious liberty, founded the first Friends

Figure 11. Newton Burial Grounds in Haddon Township. Photograph by Samuel Rhoads, 1909. Courtesy of the Camden County Historical Society Collection.

Figure 12. Concrete memorial at Newton Union Burial Ground with inset recovered headstones. Andrew Levecchia, photographer, Newton Union Burial Ground National Register of Historic Places nomination form (Trenton, NJ: New Jersey State Historic Preservation Office), photograph no. 0010. Nomination approved by the New Jersey State Review Board on July 19, 2010.

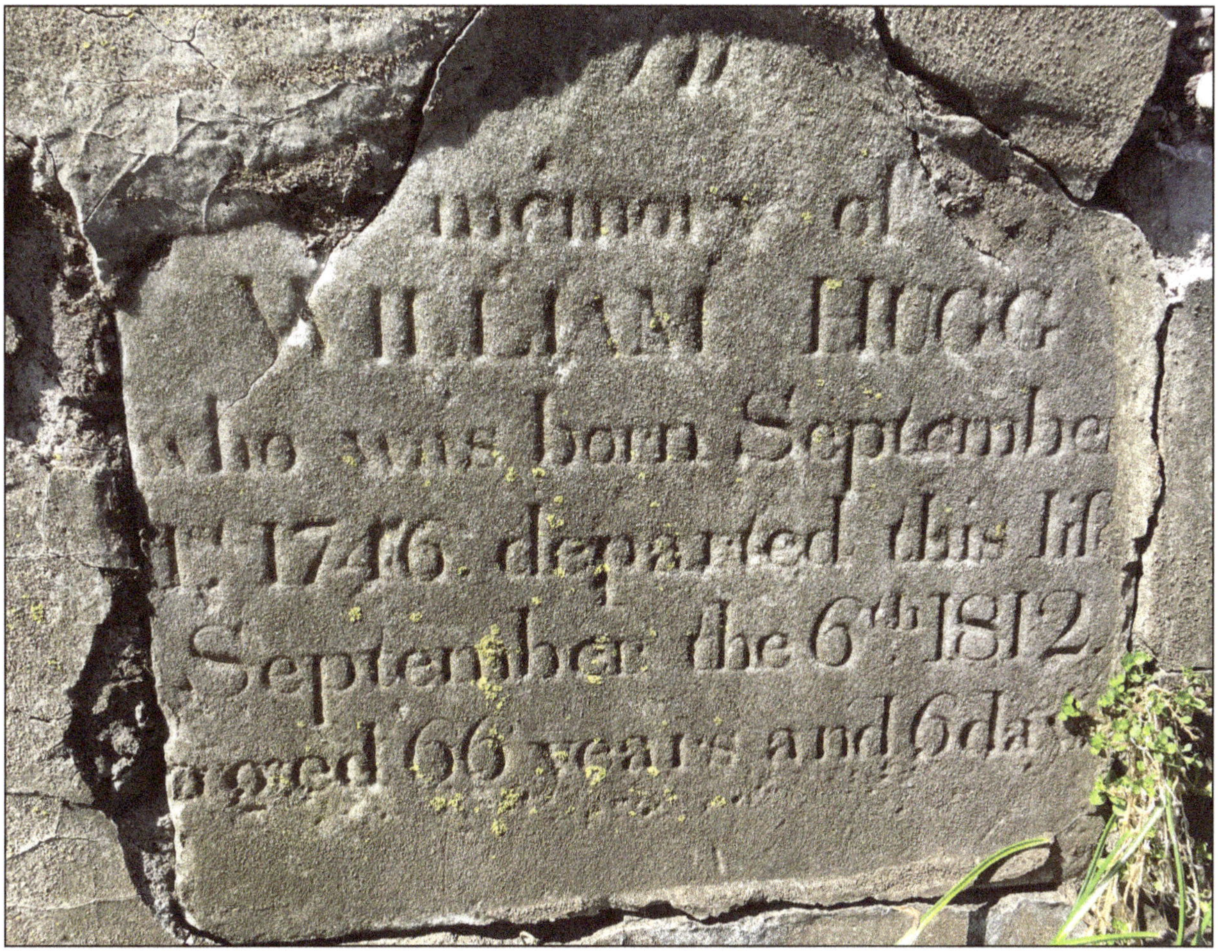

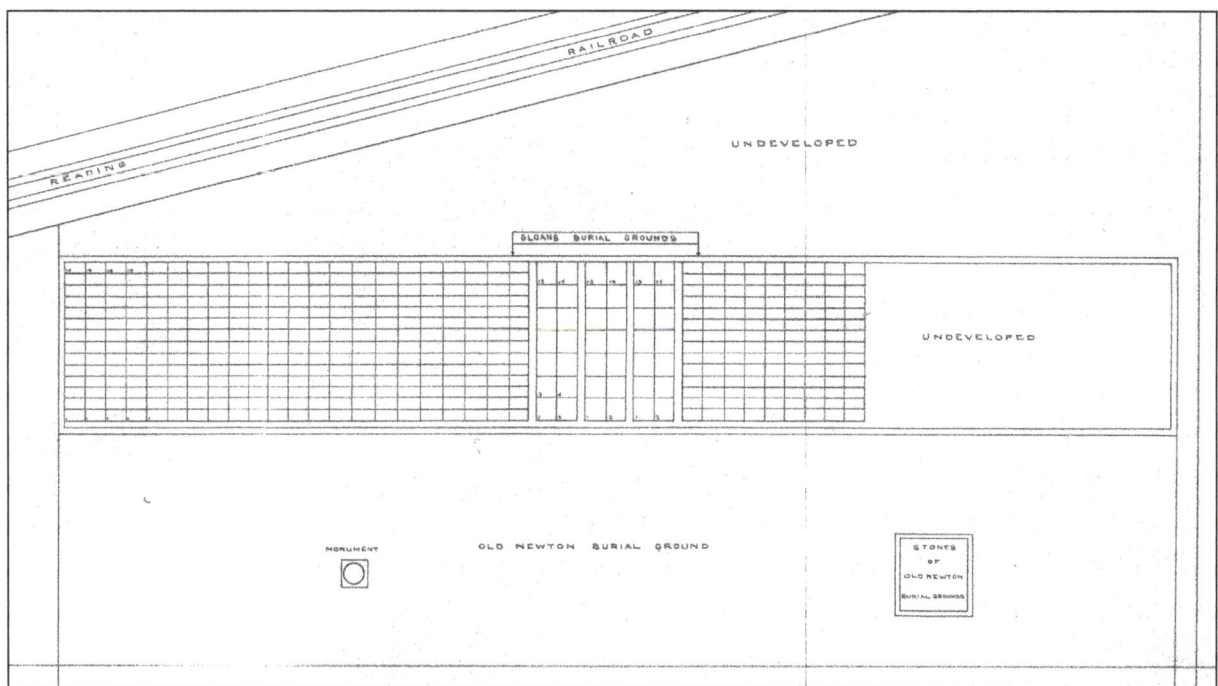

Figure 13. Headstone of William Hugg (1766–1812) embedded in concrete memorial at the Newton Union Burial Ground, Haddon Township, New Jersey. Photograph courtesy of Robert Shinn, April 2018.

Figure 14. "Sloan and Old Newton Burial Grounds, West Collingswood, New Jersey." Drawn by Walter Reeve, c. 1938, Historical Graves Survey, Project No. 334-4, Works Progress Administration.

Meeting of Old Gloucester County, held in the home of Mark Newby. Soon after William Cooper of Pyne Poynt, associated himself with this group of worshipers. The log meeting house which they build in 1684, probably stood on the adjoining premises to the north of this tablet. In this ancient burial ground rest the remains of these early spiritual pioneers, one of whom wrote that the settlement of the colony was not so much for their own tranquility, but rather for the posterity yt should be after, and that the wilderness being planted with a good seed might grow and increase to the satisfaction of the good husbandman."[97]

The locations of the "Stones of Old Newton Burial Grounds" and the monument are shown in Figure 14.

In 1937, a *Courier-Post* reporter described the Burial Grounds' condition at that time:

> Not many years was a sight to move the stoniest heart to pity. The ancient stone wall had begun to crumble, chiefly because heartless wanderers had kicked parts of it over, gouging out bricks which had been brought from England [an incorrect assertion]. Despite the high grass and weeds in those days, there was a division mark, like the bed of an old brook, but on both sides the stones, going back to the earliest 1700s, were broken and defaced by those who cared nothing for tradition and hallowed ground.[98]

Figure 15. "Nancy Eisenberg of Barrington and Virginia Bohn of Collingswood copy inscription from weathered tombstone in Newton Burial Ground, believed the oldest cemetery in South Jersey." Copyright, *Courier-Post*, May 24, 1971, 11. Reprinted with permission. All rights reserved.

Apparently, while the Friends continued to maintain their half of the burial ground, the same article indicated that the Sloan Grounds had not fared so well, since:

> ...in the other half, where the wall is still crumbling, where stones are broken across, where many markers are hidden altogether and where the long grass mingles with whatever thoughtless persons toss across the broken barrier, it is apparent that many Memorial Days have meant nothing at all. Members of the Collings family, and their kin, are buried in rows and rows.[99]

Figure 16. "John Wright, 15, sets a marker at the Sloan-Newton Burial Ground in Haddon Township." Copyright, *Courier-Post*, September 5, 1982, 15. Reprinted with permission. All rights reserved.

The Works Progress Administration (WPA) made several more attempts to restore the burial ground in 1938 and 1940. In 1939, the WPA constructed a community playground on the Northeast corner of Collings and Lynne avenues. The WPA used stones from a wall surrounding the cemetery to make a fireplace and chimney in the playground community house, a remodeled former railroad station. In September 1954, four Boy Scouts of Troop 112, sponsored by the West Collingswood Presbyterian Church, camped on and restored part of the burial ground and placed markers to identify many graves.[100] The Haddon Township Department of Public Works cleaned up the grounds and gave it the semblance of a quiet park in 1956.[101] In 1971, Ye Olde Newton Chapter of the Daughters of the American Revolution sought to have the burial ground restored through a newly formed Collingswood-Newton Colony Historical Society. The Chapter's local regent claimed that "...today, one could hardly mistake it for a park and it is anything but quiet" as the "monument erected in 1931 contains broken bottles, cigarette butts, and other trash. The walls are defaced by childish scrawls in chalk and crayon and the neighborhood youngsters climb over the stones and jump haphazardly over graves, many of which are sunken." The regent added, "Broken markers lie scattered over the burial ground, their hidden jagged edges inviting some unwary youngsters to trip over them."[102] One of the group's first projects sponsored children members of the DAR recording readable tombstones of Revolutionary War soldiers.

Marilyn Tulk, acting chairwoman of the Haddon Township Historical Society, began an effort to determine who was buried where in "perhaps one of the most historic spots in the township" in 1975. A year later, she applied for and received markers from the Veterans Administration for those Revolutionary War veterans. During the same year, the Haddonfield Friends deeded over to the Township of Haddon the original Newton and Sloan burial grounds. Four Collingswood Troop 59 Boy Scouts and their adult leader replaced 22 Revolutionary War veterans headstones at the Sloan-Newton Burial Ground[103] over Labor Day weekend in September 1982.

The Historical Societies of Haddon Township and Collingswood formally dedicated the gravestones on October 3, 1982. Four hundred people attended, including Congressman and future New Jersey Governor James J. Florio, Camden County Freeholders, State Senators, representatives of the Sons and Daughters of the American Revolution, the Society of the War of 1812, the mayors of the adjoining towns that once comprised Newton Colony, and descendants of the original settlers.

National Register of Historic Places

On July 19, 2018, the New Jersey Historic State Review Board for Historic Sites voted unanimously to recommend that the Newton Union Burial Ground be listed in the New Jersey Register of Historic Places.[104] The nomination application contains a list of those known Newton Union Burial Ground burials. It includes

Figure 17. Newton Graveyard, West Collingswood. View of lower part of graveyard from railroad embankment at the Newton Creek bridge. S. N. Rhoads, photographer, 1909.

names listed in Joseph Hinchman's *Journal* (1811–1828), in Marriage and Death Meeting Minutes of the Newton (now Haddonfield) Meeting, and on the "Find a Grave" website.[105] The aforementioned website contains 303 records under the names Newton Burying Ground, Newton Union Cemetery, and Old Newton Friends Burial Ground. The application indicated that most of the burial ground contains open space covered by turf grass with wooded areas and sporadic trees in addition to two monuments, an external wall, and approximately 117 gravestones. The total number of people buried is unknown.[106]

The burial ground is associated with an important historical event—the founding of the Newton Colony and Camden County. It is also the final resting place for some of the first political and religious leaders of West New Jersey, leaders who took an active role in establishing and maintaining religious liberty and democracy. The burial ground was the first laid out in present-day Camden County and the third in West New Jersey. The burial ground and meeting house location remains as an important reminder of the region's settlement history. Many of the county's "founding fathers" and their families met and conducted religious worship in the Meeting House on the grounds. Their children were educated and wed at the meeting house, and the colonial government administration occurred within the meetinghouse. A significant portion of the broad patterns of early colonial regional history can be traced back to the site of this burial ground and meeting house. Historian Charles S. Boyer called it "The site of Camden County's Origin" and "The Resting Place of the Early Pioneers."

While the Burial Ground is representative of the distinct characteristics of a Friends cemetery, it is also unique in holding a separate section for the remains of former Friends who left or were shunned from their meeting for failing to observe Friends' doctrine. Examples of infractions warranting separation included marrying "out of meeting" or "contrary to discipline" (i.e., marrying a non-Friend) or supporting or participating in military action. The Sloan Section holds 22 former Friends who served in the American Revolutionary War and who fought with the local militia.

The Friends now resting in the Newton Union Burial Ground believed that government was divinely instituted and that virtuous men and women must help make it operate as God intended. From the early to mid-1700s until about 1766, the descendants of these Friends controlled or greatly influenced the governments of West New Jersey and, after 1703, New Jersey.[107] Their descendants intermarried with Pennsylvania Friends, who laid out the foundations of government and governed in the Philadelphia area prior to the American Revolution. In the mid-eighteenth century, their descendants became increasingly involved in the abolition movement. Beginning in 1681, the government specified that each tenth in which settlement had occurred would be represented in the Assembly by delegates. The Irish Tenth had seven Assembly members: William Cooper, Mark Newbie, Henry Stacy, Francis Collins, Samuel Cole, Thomas Howell and William Bates. These men likely met at the site of the Newton Burial Ground in the log meeting house to discuss various issues facing the Newton Colony. These settlers also defended the right of self-government, religious liberty, and local self-determination, as judges, sheriffs, and even as soldiers.

The Newton Union Burial Ground could yield significant information important to the colonial era history of the West New Jersey and Camden County regions as it has remained largely untouched for the past three hundred years, except for gravestone removal and/or sinking and the removal of the perimeter wall. If an important reason arises to disturb the burial ground, archaeological investigations and analysis of archival records, artifacts (including garments and other personal items) and coffin/casket forms and their associated hardware could confirm the range of dates of the burials, growth of the cemetery, and changes in burial practices, the spatial organization of graves within the cemetery, and possible social differentiation among interred individuals. Ground penetrating radar (GPR) could locate most of the unmarked grave shafts and determine if more than one person occupies any of the graves.

Historic burial grounds are "oases of history in a constantly changing landscape."[108] The Newton Union Burial Ground is "a history lesson in old names and events that helped shape the future of Camden County and South Jersey."[109]

> In these burial grounds lies the venerated dust of our pioneer ancestors, they who were the bone and sinew of this part of West Jersey, patriots, who for religion's sake came across the seas, braving the wilderness to found a new nation. Knowing how well they built, shall not those of this generation, who enjoy the beauty and freedom which they left to us, see to it that this spot be kept as a monument to their zeal and patriotism?"[110]

Burial grounds are important repositories of historical information and are a physical record of a community's former inhabitants. They should serve as focal points for local history.

The Newton Union Burial Ground

About the Authors

Robert Shinn is the Treasurer of the Camden County Historical Society and co-author of *Along the Cooper River: Camden to Haddonfield,* (Arcadia, 2015). The New Jersey State Review Board for Historic Sites approved three applications for the New Jersey and National Registers he prepared: The Cooper River Park Historic District; the Peter J. McGuire Memorial and Gravesite; and the Newton Union Burial Ground. He has worked as a Petty's Island history consultant for the New Jersey National Lands Trust for the last six years, conducting history hikes and tours of the island, scripting and producing a documentary history film, and writing and narrating a self-guided audio history tour. He received his BA and Masters Degrees from Brown University. He retired as president of the Exelon Corporation's venture capital subsidiary.

Andrew Levecchia is the Director of Planning for Camden County, New Jersey, managing the daily operations of the Camden County Planning Board. He prepared the application to place the Newton Union Burial Ground on the New Jersey and National Registers of Historic Places. He received a Masters Degree in Public Administration from Rutgers University where he was awarded a fellowship from the Walter Rand Institute for Public Affairs. He studied land use and urban planning in the City of Camden. He earned a Bachelors in Geography from Rowan University and is an adjunct faculty member in Rowan's Geography, Planning and Sustainability Department. Andrew has a Professional Planners License for the State of NJ and is a member of the American Institute of Certified Planners.

Sandra White-Grear is a lifelong Haddon Township resident and serves as an officer of the Haddon Township Historical Society. She has written several articles for the Haddon Township Historical Society and the Camden County History Alliance's *Heritage* magazine. In 2011 White-Grear co-authored the book *Images of America: Haddon Township* (Arcadia Publishing).

Endnotes

1. "yt" means "that" in seventeenth-century English usage.
2. John Clement, *Sketches of the First Emigrant Settlers Newton Township Old Gloucester County, West Jersey* (Camden, NJ: Sinnickson Chew, 1877), 24.
3. Ibid., 35.
4. Other early pioneers in the Third tenth include Richard Arnold, Samuel Cole, Francis Collins, Richard Matthews, Joshua Lord, John Ladd, John Constantine, Jeremiah Wood, John Hugg, Samuel Harrison, Andrew Robeston, and Richard Bull.
5. Charles S. Boyer, *The Civil and Political History of Camden County and City* (Camden, NJ: Privately Printed, 1922), 10–11. A history of the Irish and English Friends of the Newton settlement is given in Clement, *Sketches of the First Emigrant Settlers*, and Isaac Mickle, *Reminiscences of Old Gloucester* (Philadelphia, PA: Townsend Ward, 1845), 47–50.
6. The original boundaries of the Third tenth changed after the London and Yorkshire Settlers decided to consolidate their settlements at Burlington originally planned for the Londoners at Arawames (today's Gloucester City) and Yorkshire Friends at the Falls (today's Trenton). James Wasse, William Penn's agent for West New Jersey, drew up the original plans. The land between Timber Creek and Oldman's Creek then was the original Third Tenth; see Samuel Smith, *The History of the Colony of Nova Caesaria, Or New Jersey* (Trenton, NJ, Wm. S. Sharp, 1765 [1877]), 92–98. For a discussion and explanation of why the Wasse plan for two settlements was replaced with one, see Paul W. Schopp's blog: www.jerseyman-historynowandthen.blogspot.com, "The Best Laid Schemes o' Mice an' Men, Gang aft Agley," 2010.
7. West New Jersey's Third Tenth extended along the Delaware River between the Pennsauken and Big Timber Creeks and would later be divided into Waterford, Newton, Gloucester, and Gloucestertown townships, which today roughly corresponds to Camden County.
8. "Quakers in Colonial Pennsylvania, http://www.quakersintheworld.org/quakers-in-action/282/Quakers-in-colonial-Pennsylvania.
9. Albert Cook Myers, *Immigration of the Irish Friends into Pennsylvania* (Lancaster, PA: The New Era Printing Company, 1902), 42.
10. John E. Pomfret, *Colonial New Jersey: A History* (New York: Charles Scribner's Sons, 1973), 37.
11. Magistrates persecuted Friends under the Acts of Uniformity passed by Parliament after the Restoration of Charles II.
12. This value in 1700 would roughly equal $18.4 million in 2018. Source: https://www.uwyo.edu/numimage/currency.htm.
13. Myers, *Immigration of the Irish Friends*, 42.
14. Cromwell's army had many recruits from non-conformist English sects. While most soldiers returned home after the civil war in Ireland, a number stayed as farmers on land received as payment for their military service, or, after selling their land, as shopkeepers. (Robert Dunlop, ed., *Ireland Under the Commonwealth, Documents*, 2 vols. (Manchester, 1913). These included Captain Thomas Holme from northern England, who gained experience as a landowner in County Wexford, before becoming Surveyor General of Pennsylvania, and soldier Robert Turner, from Cambridge, who became a successful linen merchant after selling his Irish lands. Audrey Lockhard, "The Friends and Emigration from Ireland to the North American Colonies," *Quaker History*. 77, no. 2 (Fall 1988), 67–92)
15. John Pomfret, *The Province of West Jersey 1609–1702*

(Princeton, NJ: Princeton University Press, 1956), 89.
16. Ibid., 121.
17. *Persecution of the Friends Digital History* ID 94, http://www.digitalhistory.uh.edu/disp_textbook.cfm?smtID=3&psid=94.
18. From August 1673 to February 1674, the Dutch again ruled New York, New Jersey, and Delaware. All returned again to Great Britain by the 1674 Treaty of Westminster.
19. Jeffry Dorwart, Camden County, NJ: *The Making of a Metropolitan Community, 1626–2000* (New Brunswick, NJ: Rutgers University Press, 2001) Kindle edition, location 162.
20. Byllynge was much abused for his faith after moving to London in 1659, including receiving beatings and rough treatment. He was prominent in efforts to obtain relief for other persecuted Friends and wrote tracts sponsoring social and political liberties.
21. Britain justified its invasion and acquisition of New Netherland chiefly by the conviction that New Netherland was purchasing tobacco in Maryland and Virginia and shipping it via New Amsterdam, thus costing the British Exchequer thousands of pounds sterling annually and the English merchants unnecessary loss of trade. In July 1663, the Council of Foreign Plantations, Sir John Berkeley presiding, appointed a special committee consisting of himself, Sir George Carteret, and William Coventry, secretary to James, Duke of York, to inquire into the feasibility of taking New Netherland. In January it reported that the seizure could be effected at small cost. The Duke was highly pleased, since, as a large holder in the Royal African Company, he was interested in crippling the Dutch. (Pomfret, *The Province of West Jersey*, 52). Charles granted New Jersey to James, the duke of York. James granted it to Sir George Carteret and Sir John Berkeley.
22. Pomfret, *The Province of West Jersey*, 66.
23. The duke of York initially refused to recognize the transaction because, though granted amnesty, Fenwick most likely had been at the head of Cromwell's cavalry at the execution of the duke's father. Penn and the other trustees smoothed relations with the crown, divided the territory of West New Jersey into one hundred proprietary shares and granted Fenwick ten.
24. Ibid.
25. Pomfret, *The Province of West Jersey*, 86
26. Pomfret, *Colonial New Jersey*, 1973, 41.
27. Pomfret, *The Province of West Jersey*, 970.
28. A right to a fractional division of the proprietorship of the colony, and the basis for voting rights in the General Board or Council. Sometimes, but not exclusively, used to mean a full share (i.e., 1/100th in West Jersey). West Jersey—the western division was partitioned into tenths, with one tenth granted to John Fenwick. The other nine tenths of West Jersey were then divided again into tenths producing ninety hundredth parts. These shares, or proprieties, were then divided into smaller parts. Some shares were divided into sevenths (i.e., 1/7 of 1/90) and initially valued at £50—an affordable price for many investors. Many of the shares were divided into 1/32 parts, and this became the minimum holding required for a shareholder to be entitled to a proprietary voting right. Source: Joseph R. Klett, "Using the Records of the East and West Jersey Proprietors," New Jersey Archives, 2014. Accessed 3/5/2018 at https://www.nj.gov/state/archives/pdf/proprietors.pdf.
29. The proprietor group which purchased one whole West Jersey propriety (1/100th of West Jersey) included Dublin Friends Robert Turner, Robert Zane, Thomas Thackara, William Bates, and Joseph Sleigh and County Wickloe Friend, William Bates. George R. Prowell, *The History of Camden County, New Jersey* (Philadelphia, PA: L. J. Richards & Co., 1886), 638–40.
30. Pomfret, *The Province of West Jersey*, 90.
31. Zane, then a young man, was the pioneer of the Newton settlement, having sailed to West Jersey four years before, probably in the same ship John Fenwick hired. Zane remained in constant correspondence with Robert Turner, the major force behind organizing and financing the undertaking. Promfret, *he Province of West Jersey*, 123. ". . . beginning of the year 1682, we all removed from Salem together with Robert Zane, that had been settled there, who came along from Ireland with the Thompsons before hinted, and having expectation of our coming only bought a lot in Salem own, upon which he seated himself until our coming, whose proprietary right and our being of the same nature, could not then take it up in Fenwick's Tenth, and so we began our settlement." Isaac Mickle, *Reminiscences of Old Gloucester*, 48 quoting Thomas Sharp.
32. Cooper "had been settled some time before" a meeting was set up and kept at the house of Mark Newbie. Isaac Mickle, *Reminiscences of Old Gloucester*, 48.
33. King Charles II granted Penn a royal charter for his new colony on March 4, 1681—seven months before the five sailed from Dublin. Penn sent his cousin, William Markham, ahead of Penn's own planned departure, to act as Deputy Governor and to find land that met Penn's specifications for Philadelphia. Markham and Thomas Fairman, one of his councilors, began a seven weeks survey of alternate sites in October 1681. They selected the area on the Delaware's west bank above the marshes at the mouth of the Schuylkill for the future location of Philadelphia. This included the northern third of the Swansons' 1,145 acres that had been surveyed the previous June and was still unimproved.
34. "To be near this growing place, Robert no doubt, considered desirable; and when his friends arrived from Ireland, he called their attention to these advantages, and, through his representations, the place on the north bank of Newton Creek was fixed upon and an embryo town soon build." Clement, *Sketches of the First Emigrant Settlers Newton Township*, 13.
35. Charles S. Boyer, *The Civil and Political History of Camden County and City* (Camden, NJ: Privately Printed, 1922), 10.

The Newton Union Burial Ground

36 William Bates' land would later become Oaklyn, New Jersey.

37 Prowell, *The History of Camden County*, 650. "The name, Newton, does not appear in early records but some historians say that it was originally named for Sir Isaac Newton, famous English mathematician and philosopher —the father of gravity. Others say the work is derived from New Towne." Raymond Mitchell Bancroft, *Collingswood Story: A Series of Chapter Profiles in Picture and Story* (Collingswood, NJ: n.p., 1965), 9.

38 Prowell, *History of Camden County*, 650.

39 Between Mark Newbie's house and what is now the White Horse Pike, Thomas Thackara built his home facing the creek. There is a Thackara house there now, numbered 912 Eldridge Avenue, Collingswood, NJ. It faces the creek and carries the letters I T M and the date 1714. It probably is on the site of the original Thomas Thackara house. http://www.dvrbs.com/camden-texts/CamdenNJ-CCHS-Upper410.htm.

40 Charles Boyer wrote that the meeting house "formerly stood near the graveyard adjacent to the West Collingswood Station on the Philadelphia and Reading Railroad." *The Civil and Political History of Camden County and City*, 17. While Boyer's map shows a suggested meeting house location, the specific footprint of the original Newton Meetinghouse has yet to be identified. The text of a bronze tablet placed at the foot of an historical monument installed in the burial ground by the Camden County Historical Society in 1931 states: "The log meeting house which they built in 1684 probably stood on the adjoining premises to the north of this tablet."

41 "History Uncovered and Relived As Playground is Established," *Courier-Post*, August 3, 1939, 17.

42 The earliest Salem Meeting occurred in a dedicated building (i.e., not someone's residence) in 1681, the year Samuel and Ann Nicholson gave their log house and sixteen surrounding acres to the Salem Meeting (Pomfret, *The Province of West Jersey*, 22). Francis Collins completed the first Burlington Meeting House in 1693. Robert L. Thompson, *A History of Burlington, New Jersey, Told Through the Lives and Times of its People* (Galloway, NJ: South Jersey Culture & History Center, 2016), 24.

43 In the first two decades of the eighteenth century, Quaker families migrated southward from Burlington and eastward from Newton, an activity accelerated with road building, commercial development, and the arrival of Elizabeth Haddon, making Haddonfield an important Quaker settlement. http://www.haddonfieldfriendsmeeting.org/wordpress/?page_id=80.

44 In 1760, a new Meeting House constructed of brick replaced the 1721 Meeting House.

45 Atlantic City R. R. Co., *Plan Showing Part to be Acquired of Private "Union" Burying Ground, September 25, 1925*.

46 Sandra White-Grear, *Settlement of Newton Township, Champion School, and Newton Burial Grounds History plus Notes On A Typical One Room Schoolhouse Routine*. Compiled for the Haddon Township Historical Society, February 8, 2015 from the notes of Alfred Litwak, caretaker and docent of the Champion School, 1986–2014. Source: https://www.facebook.com/friendsofthechampionschool/posts/settlement-of-newton-township-champion-school-and-newton-burial-grounds-historyp/783797611704498/ accessed on October 15, 2018."

47 Prowell, *The History of Camden County*, 650. Friends tended to bury family members in clusters—a pattern showing to some extent in the better documented "Sloan section" of the Newton Union Burial Ground and in the Haddonfield Meeting graveyard.

48 According to the Haddonfield Monthly Meeting website, "Around 1715 Newton Meeting moved from its site along Newton Creek to Haddonfield and changed its name to Haddonfield Monthly Meeting." http://www.haddonfieldfriendsmeeting.org/wordpress/?page_id=80. An inventory of 794 gravesites listing the names, birth and death dates, and other information is maintained by the Haddonfield Monthly meeting at http://www.haddonfieldfriendsmeeting.org/wordpress/wp-content/uploads/2011/01/HMM-graveyard-inventory.pdf. The inventory indicates three members buried at the Newton Burial Ground.

49 Newton Friends Meeting House dates to c.1801 on ground Joseph Kaighn donated at the corner of Mt. Vernon Street and Mt. Ephraim Avenue in Camden and remained in use until 1957. According to the Federal Writers' Project, it was the first house of worship in Camden. It was a two-and-one-half-story rectangular building, of post-Colonial design, constructed of red brick with white trim. Friends met there until 1915. In 1935, WPA funded restoration of the building under the direction of the Camden County Historical Society.

50 Clement, *Sketches of the First Emigrant Settlers Newton Township*, contains short biographies of the most prominent members of 38 families who made up the first emigrant settlers, including their civic and religious contributions in the early years of the West Jersey Province.

51 From a 1908 address Mr. Augustus Reeve delivered in 1921 to the Camden Historical Society, as reported in Ben Courter's, "Torchlight Funeral of Long Ago," *Courier-Post*, February 2, 1931, 10. There are other strong indicators that the emigrant William Cooper was buried at the Newton burying ground in addition to the histories of Howard Cooper and George Prowell. First, no other nearby burial ground then existed, as Haddonfield Meeting dates to after 1720. Second, no less than seven of his close relatives are listed as having been buried in the "Burying Ground at Newton" in the Newton Meeting Minutes, including Joshua Cooper (1727), William Cooper (1727), Mary Cooper (1728), Lydia Cooper (1731), Joseph Cooper (1733), Lucia Cooper (1736) Joseph Cooper (1791), and Elizabeth Cooper (date illegible). Further, Benjamin B. Cooper is interred in Sloan's yard adjacent. Other records indicate that Sara Cooper, Benjamin B. Cooper's wife (1824), and Benjamin Cooper's son (1818), are also buried

in the Newton Grave Yard.

52 Sharp's 1700 map of Newton and other areas of the West Jersey Province serve as the best and only accurate record of local land boundaries and roads.

53 Sharp's history is copied from Liber A, of Gloucester deeds, page 98, in the office of the Secretary of State, at Trenton, NJ, and reproduced in Clement, *Sketches of the First Emigrant Settlers Newton Township*, 24–26.

54 Part of the site later became a ferry terminal the Cooper family operated, who then sold the franchise to the Camden & Atlantic Railroad. Ferry service ended at Coopers Point in October 1926, just two months after the Delaware River Bridge (now the Benjamin Franklin Bridge) opened for traffic.

55 Clement, *Sketches of the First Emigrant Settlers Newton Township*, 152.

56 Clement, *Sketches of the First Emigrant Settlers Newton Township*, 37.

57 These coins, known as "St. Patrick's half pence"—with the words "Floreat Rex" on the obverse and "Ecce Rex" on the reverse—were probably intended simply to commemorate that event and not circulated as money in Ireland.

58 Newbie's coins apparently continued to circulate for some time, when, having served their purpose, they were called in and redeemed.

59 Richard Francis Veit and Mark Nonestied, *New Jersey Cemeteries and Tombstones: History of the Landscape* (New Brunswick, NJ: Rutgers University Press, 1968), 20.

60 Ibid.

61 For more information on Quaker burying grounds and Funerary practices, see Lisa Arnold's post "Gonna Lay This Body Down: Quaker Funerals & Burials, https://blogs.ancestry.com/ancestry/2014/06/07/gonna-lay-this-body-down-quaker-funerals-burials/ and her book *Thee & Me: A Beginner's Guide to Early Quaker Records* (self published, 2014). For details and maps of "Quaker Burial Grounds in Philadelphia from 1683 to Present," visit Swarthmore College's http://www.swarthmore.edu/library/friends/philaburials3.htm.

62 *Rules of Discipline and Christian Advices* (Philadelphia: Samuel Sansom, Jun., 1797), 59.

63 Veit, et al., *New Jersey Cemeteries and Tombstones*, 114.

64 This practice continues today. Based on the long-standing practice of Salem Monthly Meeting, confirmed by Monthly Meeting on 16, first month, 2005: the burial ground is an ongoing public statement of our testimonies on simplicity, equality and integrity. In accordance with our book of discipline entitled Faith and Practice, "Friends have traditionally expressed their commitments to simplicity and the equality of all persons by discouraging the use of elaborate grave markers. Graves should be marked by plain stones that bear only the name of the deceased and dates of birth and death." In keeping with the size and scale of the existing stones, monuments located in the cemetery are not to exceed the following dimensions: 18 inches tall by 24 inches wide by 12 inches deep. Monuments that mark a double plot may be up to 36 inches wide. The design of all monuments should be an expression of simplicity in both detail and text. Shape is limited to a rectangular or slightly rounded top. http://salemmeeting.org/graveyard/.

65 London Yearly Meeting (Society of Friends), *Book of Christine Discipline of the Religious Society of Friends in Great Britain* (London: Samuel Harris & Co., 1883), 165.

66 Dennis Raible, *Down a Country Lane* (Camden, NJ: Camden County Historical Society, 1998), 84.

67 Douglas B. Rauschenberger and Katherine Mansfield Tassini, *Lost Haddonfield* (Haddonfield, NJ: The Historical Society of Haddonfield, 1999), 124.

68 Jerry William Frost, *The Quaker Family in Colonial America*, (London: St. Martin's Press, 2014), 43.

69 "History Uncovered and Relived As Playground is Established," *Courier-Post*, August 3, 1939, 17.

70 Esther Saxby and Richard Thacakara, Thomas Thackara's son.

71 Clement, *Sketches of the First Emigrant Settlers Newton Township*, 296–97.

72 The first significant schism among Friends in the American colonies occurred in the Philadelphia area in 1692–93. The Friends holding the reins of power in Penn's colony successfully suppressed George Keith followers. They had Keith and several supporters arrested and prosecuted for sedition. The jury failed to convict, but the Keithians lost momentum. During the American Revolution, some pro-Independence Friends (such as Betsy Ross and General Nathanael Greene) were read out of their meetings. When the war was over, many more left the Society of Friends in the face of widespread feeling that Quakers had favored the British side, according to Kevin Phillips, *The Cousins' Wars* (Basic Books, 1998), 211–17 and 643–44, fn. 68. http://www.strecorsoc.org/docs/fracture.html. Those who supported the war organized their own Friends' Meeting in 1783, known as "The Free Quaker Meeting" and located at 5th and Arch in Philadelphia.

73 "Elias Hicks," *The Encyclopedia of Greater Philadelphia*, https://philadelphiaencyclopedia.org/archive/religious-society-of-friends-quakers/3b44203v/.

74 Walter D. Joyce, unaddressed letter, Collingswood, April 27, 1950, states that it was a "marble stone tablet set in the old brick wall that divided the Private 'Union Burying Ground from the Burial Ground of Ancient Newton Meeting."

75 Charles S. Boyer, "Camden County Gravestones—Sloan or Union Burying Ground, West Collingswood," *The Genealogical Magazine of New Jersey*, Vol. IX, No. 3, July–October 1934, 89–93.

76 Ibid.

77 Including Eastlack, Collins, Hinchman, Albertson, Knight, Evaul, Cooper, Strafford, Sloan, Champion, Thackara, Lee, Foster, Dill, and Gilmore. Many of these surnames live on as local street names. See "Settlement of Newton Township, Champion School, and Newton Burial Grounds History plus Notes On A

Typical One Room Schoolhouse Routine" (Compiled by Sandra White-Grear, Haddon Township Historical Society, February 8, 2015, from the notes of Alfred Litwak, caretaker and docent of the Champion School, 1986–2014, and other sources, accessed at https://www.facebook.com/friendsofthechampionschool/posts/settlement-of-newton-township-champion-school-and-newton-burial-grounds-historyp/783797611704498/.

78 Thomas Bergbauer, "Cemetery a Lesson in Names, Events that Shaped County," *Courier-Post*, March 11, 2004, 15.

79 Ibid.

80 Melvina Oehlers of the Princeton Chapter of the Daughters of the American Revolution compiled this list.

81 Ibid. Others sources included David C. Munn, NJ State Library, and research efforts of a group in 1924 from Marilyn Tulk personal files. These include Captain John Davis (1757–1828), Jamie Colter, 6th Class (1743–1811), James Hall, 3rd Class (????–1822), Robert Bryant (1765–Unknown), Josiah and John Shivers, Captain Robert Maddox, Joseph Brown, Richard Bickham, and Caleb Bickham.

82 *Camden Democrat*, October 29, 1859, 2.

83 The Camden County Board of Freeholders and Camden County Historical Society sponsored the WPA *Historical Graves Survey* for the two burial grounds.

84 Including John Dill, John Thackara, John Davis, James Sloan, Jacob Albertson, Joseph Albertson, Isaac Albertson, Joseph Collings, Edward Collings, Jacob Evaul, and John Heritage.

85 The Newton Creek and its south branch was the border of two former townships after whom the burial ground was renamed. Union Township existed from 1831 to 1868 in present-day Camden County, New Jersey. When the legislature separated Camden County from Gloucester County in 1844, Union Township was one of the original Camden County municipalities. In 1855, state lawmakers erected a new township, Centre Township, from Union Township's landmass, and, in 1868, the state dissolved Union township and the remaining land became Gloucester City. Newton Township existed within Gloucester County from its creation in 1695, and became part of Camden County in 1844, where it existed until 1871. Current municipalities that were formerly part of Newton Township include Haddon Township, Camden, Collingswood, Audubon, Haddonfield and Pennsauken Township. Source: *Wikipedia*, https://en.wikipedia.org/wiki/Newton_Township,_Camden_County,_New_Jersey Accessed on October 15, 2018.

86 According to Joseph Hinchman, in *Joseph Hinchman's Diary* (New Jersey: Sarah Fenimore Collings/Mrs. Ruth Cross Triol, 1983).

87 Champion's wife, Elizabeth Zane Champion, was a direct descendant of Robert Zane.

88 Margaret Westfield, *Newton Union School House/ Champion School National Register of Historic Places Inventory— Nomination Form*, February 25, 1988.

89 Prowell, *The History of Camden County*, 650.

90 For the history of the Atlantic City Railroad and its related companies, see W. George Cook and William J. Coxey, *Atlantic City Railroad, The Royal Route to the Sea: A History of the Reading's Seashore Railroad, 1877–1933* (Oaklyn, NJ: National Railway Historical Society, 1980).

91 Dennis Raible, *Down a Country Lane*, 83.

92 "The Old Newton Burial Grounds," *West Jersey Press*, April 14, 1927, 1.

93 "Moving of Old Tombstones Called 'Historical Outrage,'" *Courier-Post*, May 12, 1931, 1–2.

94 Ibid.

95 Ibid.

96 From notes on large map of Newton Burial Ground by Charles Boyer 1934 on wall of the Champion School, courtesy of Sandra White Grear.

97 Ben Courter, "Where Early Settlers Lie," *Courier-Post*, October 30, 1933, 8. Quotation taken from Sharp's account as reported in Isaac Mickle, *Reminiscences of Old Gloucester*, 49.

98 Henry C. Beck, "Weeds Mar Beauty of Old Burial Ground, *Courier-Post*, July 3, 1937, 3.

99 Ibid.

100 "Boy Scouts Busy Cleaning Up Old Burial Ground," *Courier-Post*, September 8, 1954, 4.

101 Tom Lounsberry, "It's Resurrection Day at Newton Burial Ground," *Courier-Post*, May 24, 1971, 11.

102 Ibid.

103 Bob Reichenback, "Put to Rest—Volunteers Replacing headstones" and "Revolutionary War Dead Get New Grave Markers," *Courier-Post*, September 5, 1982, 1B and 18.

104 The New Jersey State Review Board found that the Burial Ground is significant under National Register Criteria A, C, and D. More information about the Board, National Register criteria, and the process for listing an historic site is available at https://www.nj.gov/dep/hpo/1identify/nrsr.htm.

105 "Newton Burial Ground Memorials," Findagrave.com, https://www.findagrave.com/cemetery/1275992/memorial-search?page=4#sr-184680632.

106 The largest single list includes 303 names and known birth/death dates at the Find a Grave website, www.findagrave.com.

107 Richard Matlack Cooper (1768–1843) is the most locally significant descendant of the founding families interred at the Newton Burial Ground. He held the following public offices: Gloucester county coroner, (1795–99); judge and justice of Gloucester County courts (1803–23); member of the New Jersey State General Assembly (1807–18); president of the New Jersey State Bank, (1813–42); and member of the Twenty-first and Twenty-second United States Congresses (1829–1833).

108 Richard F. Veit, et al., *New Jersey Cemeteries and Tombstones*.

109 Thomas Bergbauer, "Cemetery a Lesson in Names, Events that Shaped County."

110 West Jersey Press, "The Old Newton Burial Grounds," 1.

Recent SJCHC Publications

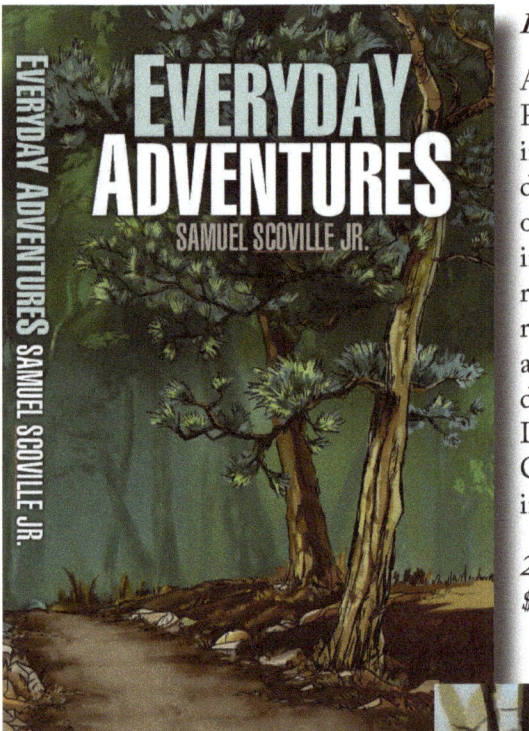

Everyday Adventures by Samuel Scoville Jr.

A collection of twelve artful essays that describe Philadelphia attorney Samuel Scoville Jr.'s jaunts into nature with arresting detail. Readers are introduced to hibernating mammals, snakes, orchids, and other flora, but especially to birds. Whether listening to birdsong, searching for hidden nests (which remain undisturbed), or quietly observing avian daily routines, Scoville describes his surroundings vividly, and often with considerable wit. He recounts expeditions in Connecticut, the Berkshires, Pennsylvania, Delaware, the Pine Barrens, and the far north of Canada. Quickly, readers find that they have stepped into the stories for everyday adventures of their own.

252 pages, paperback. ISBN: 978-0-9976699-9-2. $8.95

The Out of Doors Club by Samuel Scoville Jr.

In our second offering of Scoville's work, this collection of essays introduce the adventures of the "Band," young siblings led on imagination-filled hikes by their father. In these twenty brief essays, many set in the Pine Barrens of New Jersey, Samuel Scoville Jr. reminds readers of simpler times, when the world held fewer cares and nature walks with a parent could be the highlight of a day. Trekking through fields, bogs and forests, canoeing down rivers, the Band learn amusing lessons about nature and life. Readers, meanwhile, will appreciate the gentle and loving relationship depicted between father, mother and children.

147 pages, paperback. ISBN: 978-1-947889-90-3. $8.95

A Century Later:
The Spanish Flu in New Jersey

Brendan Honick

While the Spanish Influenza pandemic lasted from 1918 to 1920, it mainly affected New Jersey in its second wave, during the fall of 1918. This influenza strain killed an estimated 8,000 people in the state (out of 675,000 nationally). Returning World War I servicemen spread the disease, which they had contracted on the battlefields of Western Europe. In the cities, overcrowded slums expedited the contagion's dissemination. The map below depicts how the Spanish Flu affected cities, military installations, and shore towns in New Jersey.

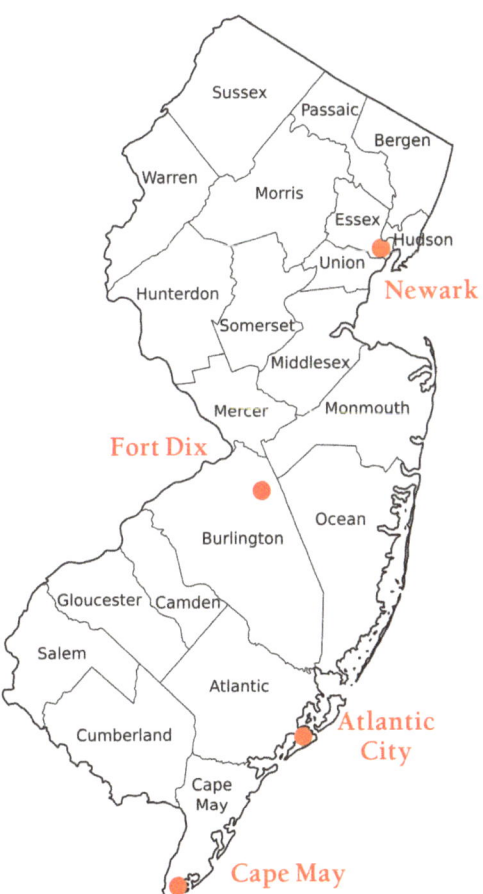

Fort Dix

Fort Dix, originally known as Camp Dix, was an important Army base during World War I. It was the training and staging ground for the 34th, 78th, and 87th divisions. The Spanish Flu took hold in mid-September 1918. From September 18 to September 19, over a thousand cases developed, and dozens were dead. By September 23, the camp was placed under quarantine: soldiers were forbidden from leaving and only officials could enter. This YMCA postcard, circa 1918, depicts soldiers at Fort Dix getting inoculation shots. At this point in medicine, viruses (e.g., the Spanish Flu) had not yet been discovered, so immunization attempts like this proved fruitless.

Life at Camp Dix, New Jersey. Innoculation. *Courtesy of the Springfield College Archives and Special Collections.*

Cape May

Since the federal government realized that Cape May was an important defensive position, it established two bases in the resort town during the Great War. One was Camp Wissahickon, and the other was Naval Section Base 9 (the site of the modern Coast Guard base). This photograph portrays some of the housing for soldiers at Camp Wissahickon, where 8,000 soldiers trained. Returning soldiers, housed in dormitories like these, carried the Spanish Flu with them from Europe.

Camp Wissahickon, U. S. Naval Training Station. Cape May, New Jersey. Company Street. *Postcard courtesy of the Paul W. Schopp collection.*

Newark

The Spanish Flu hit Newark especially hard: 29,000 people suffered from the disease in 1918, with approximately 2,200 fatalities. Charles P. Gillen, Newark's mayor, caused a scandal during the pandemic. The New Jersey Board of Health issued a statewide order to close all places of amusement, congregation, and public gathering on October 5. However, Gillen allowed businesses like saloons to remain open and for parades to occur. This carelessness caused the Spanish Flu to spread extensively in the city, which was tightly packed factory workers for the war effort. This photograph of the packed armistice parade in November 1918 shows how easy it was for the pandemic to spread.

Atlantic City

The Spanish Flu affected all aspects of life in Atlantic City. Only emergency telephone calls could be placed. The city's doctors commonly prescribed ineffective medicine, such as nasal antiseptics and alcohol. Social gatherings were canceled, and amusement parks and theaters were closed indefinitely. This sketch by James Fox shows the Atlantic City Municipal Hospital, where many victims of the Spanish Flu were treated.

Atlantic City Hospital. *Image from the* Annual Report of the Atlantic City Hospital, 1920.

About the Author

Brendan Honick is a senior at Stockton University pursuing a B.A. in Liberal Studies with a concentration in Analytical Writing. This article was originally part of an exhibition shown in the Bjork Library, Stockton University during fall 2018.

A bird's-eye view of Newark's Armistice Day Celebration, November 11, 1918. *Courtesy of the Newark Public Library.*

The Youthful Emigrant:
A True Story of the Early Settlement of New Jersey

Lydia Maria Child, with introductory remarks by Sarah Holt

Elizabeth Haddon Estaugh is considered by many to be the founder and namesake of Haddonfield, New Jersey. Recountings of her "founding" have often conflated legend with history[1] and are based mostly on local folklore. It is this nineteenth-century folklore that inspired Lydia Maria Child's story "The Youthful Emigrant." First published in 1845,[2] Child's story cemented the oral tradition of Haddon's life and popular ideas about Haddon's biography. As skillfully told as the story may be, Child's version of Haddon's journey to America and life in West New Jersey is more fiction than fact.

Local historians Elizabeth Lyons, her brother Stuart Lyons, and Professor Emeritus of History at Rutgers University-Camden Jeffrey M. Dowart have uncovered the truth about Haddon's life through dedicated reasearch. Haddon did not choose to come to America of her own volition, as depicted in Child's story. Her father requested that she settle on his purchased land and act as his real estate agent.[3] When Elizabeth arrived in 1701, there was an existing Quaker community with farms, court houses and jails.[4] No records exist of interactions between Haddon and the Lenape natives. In fact, only a few hundred Lenape remained in situ after being exposed to smallpox from the arrival of European settlers.[5] There is also no evidence of a grand romantic proposal to her husband, John Estaugh. Haddon took the initiative to arrange a marriage with her acquaintance in order to shed her spinster identity and become respected as a married woman in the Quaker community.[6] They married a year after her arrival. It is doubtful that the town was named after her, since Haddon signed every letter and legal document with the last name Estaugh for the remaining 60 years of her life in New Jersey.[7] Still, Haddon and her family used their wealth to expand the Quaker settlement that is now known as Haddonfield.[8]

"The Youthful Emigrant" is an important text that has inevitably shaped local culture, despite its historical inaccuracies. Child's story preserved the legend of Elizabeth Haddon originally passed down through oral tradition from generation to generation. If this folklore had not been written down, the remnants of Haddon's story and her founding of Haddonfield would have been lost.

Child's story is republished here from its inclusion in *Fact and Fiction: A Collection of Short Stories* (1846).

Friends Meeting house in Haddonfield, New Jersey, 1844.

THE YOUTHFUL EMIGRANT

A being breathing thoughtful breath;
A traveller betwixt life and death;
The reason firm, the temperate will,
Endurance, foresight, strength and skill.
A perfect woman, nobly planned,
To warn, to comfort, and command;
And yet a spirit still, and bright
With something of an angel light.—
                    WORDSWORTH

The latter part of the seventeenth century saw rapid accessions to the Society of Friends, called Quakers. The strong humility, the indwelling life, which then characterised that peculiar sect, attracted large numbers, even of the wealthy, to its unworldly doctrines. Among these were John Haddon and his wife Elizabeth, well-educated and genteel people, in the city of London. Like William Penn, and other proselytes from the higher classes, they encountered much ridicule and opposition from relatives, and the grossest misrepresentations from the public. But this, as usual, only made the unpopular faith more dear to those who had embraced it for conscience' sake.

The three daughters of John Haddon received the best education then bestowed on gentlewomen, with the exception of ornamental accomplishments. The spinnet and mandolin, on which their mother had played with considerable skill, were of course banished; and her gay embroidery was burned, lest it should tempt others to a like expenditure of time. The house was amply furnished, but with the simplest patterns and the plainest colours. An atmosphere of kindness pervaded the whole establishment, from father and mother down to the little errand-boy; a spirit of perfect gentleness, unbroken by any freaks of temper, or outbursts of glee; as mild and placid as perpetual moonlight.

The children, in their daily habits, reflected an image of home, as children always do. They were quiet, demure, and orderly, with a touch of quaintness in dress and behaviour. Their playthings were so well preserved, that they might pass in good condition to the third generation; no dogs' ears were turned in their books, and the moment they came from school, they carefully covered their little plain bonnets from dust and flies. To these subduing influences was added the early consciousness of being pointed at as peculiar; of having a cross to bear, a sacred cause to sustain.

Elizabeth, the oldest daughter, was by nature strong, earnest, and energetic, with warm affections, uncommon powers of intellect, and a lively imagination. The exact equal pressure on all sides, in strict Quaker families, is apt to produce too much uniformity of character; as the equal pressure of the air makes one globule of shot just like another. But in this rich young soul, the full stream, which under other circumstances might have overleaped safe barriers, being gently hemmed in by high banks, quietly made for itself a deeper and wider channel, and flowed on in all its fulness. Her countenance in some measure indicated this. Her large clear blue eye "looked out honest and friendly into the world," and there was an earnest seriousness about her mouth, very unusual in childhood. She was not handsome; but there was something extremely pleasing in her fresh healthy complexion, her bright intelligent expression, and her firm elastic motions.

She early attracted attention as a very peculiar child. In her usual proceedings, her remarks, and even in her play, there was a certain individuality. It was evident that she never *intended* to do anything strange. She was original merely because she unconsciously acted out her own noble nature, in her own free and quiet way. It was a spontaneous impulse with her to relieve all manner of distress. One day, she brought home a little half-blind kitten in her bosom, which her gentle eloquence rescued from cruel boys, who had cut off a portion of its ears. At another time, she asked to have a large cake baked for her, because she wanted to invite some little girls. All her small funds were expended for oranges and candy on this occasion. When the time arrived, her father and mother were much surprised to see her lead in six little ragged beggars. They were, however, too sincerely humble and religious to *express* any surprise. They treated the forlorn little ones very tenderly, and freely granted their daughter's request to give them some of her books and playthings at parting. When they had gone, the good mother quietly said, "Elizabeth, why didst thou invite strangers, instead of thy schoolmates?"

There was a heavenly expression in her eye, as she looked up earnestly, and answered, "Mother, I wanted to invite *them*, they looked *so* poor."

The judicious parents made no circumstance of it, lest it should create a diseased love of being praised for kindness. But they gave each other an expressive glance, and their eyes filled with tears; for this simple and natural action of their child seemed to them full of Christian beauty.

Under such an education, all good principles and genial impulses grew freely and took vigorous root; but the only opening for her active imagination to spread its wings, was in the marvellous accounts she heard of America and the Indians. When she was five or six years old, William Penn visited her father's house, and described some of his adventures in the wilderness, and his interviews with red men. The intelligent child eagerly devoured every word, and kept drawing nearer and nearer, till she laid her head upon his knees, and gazed into his face. Amused by her intense curiosity, the good man took her in his lap, and told her how the squaws made baskets and embroidered moccasons; how they called a baby a *pappoos*, and put him in a birch-bark cradle, which they swung on the boughs of trees. The little girl's eyes sparkled, as she inquired, "And didst thou ever see a *pappoos*-baby thyself? And hast thou got a moccason-shoe?"

"I have seen them myself, and I will send thee a moccason," he replied; "but thou mayst go to thy mother now, for I have other things to speak of."

That night, the usually sedate child scampered across the bed-room with but one sleeve of her nightgown on, and tossed up her shoe, shouting, "Ho, ho! Friend Penn is going to send me an Indian moccason! Mother, art thou glad? Hannah, art thou glad?"

This unwonted ebullition was not rebuked in words, but it soon subsided under the invisible influence of unvarying calmness.

From that time, a new character was given to all her plays. Her doll was named Pocahontas, and she swung her kitten in a bit of leather, and called it a *pappoos*. If she could find a green bough, she stuck it in the ground for a tree, placed an earthen image under it for William Penn, and sticks with feathers on them for Indian chiefs. Then, with amusing gravity of manner, she would unfold a bit of newspaper and read what she called Friend Penn's treaty with the red men. Her sisters, who were of a far less adventurous spirit, often said, "We are tired of always playing Indian. Why not play keep school, or go to see grandfather?"

But Elizabeth would answer, "No; let us play that we all go settle in America. Well, now suppose we are in the woods, with great, great, big trees all round us, and squirrels running up and down, and wolves growling."

"I don't like wolves," said little Hannah, "they will bite thee. Father says they will bite."

"I shouldn't be afraid," replied the elder sister; "I would run into the house and shut the door, when they came near enough for me to see their eyes. Here are plenty of sticks. Let us build a house; a *wigwam*, I mean. Oh, dear me, how I should love to go to America! There must be such grand great woods to run about in; and I should love to swing the little *pappooses* in the trees."

When Elizabeth was eleven years old, she went with her parents to Yearly Meeting, and heard, among other preachers, a young man seventeen years of age, named John Estaugh. He was a new proselyte, come from Essex county, to join the annual assembly of the Friends. Something in his preaching arrested the child's attention, and made a strong impression on her active mind. She often quoted his words afterwards, and began to read religious books with great diligence. John Haddon invited the youth home to dine, but as there was no room at the table for the children, Elizabeth did not see him. Her father afterward showed her an ear of Indian corn, which John Estaugh had given him. He had received several from an uncle settled in New England, and he brought some with him to London as curiosities. When the little girl was informed that the magnificent plant grew taller than herself, and had very large waving green leaves, and long silken tassels, she exclaimed, with renewed eagerness, "Oh, how I do wish I could go to America!"

Years passed on, and as the child had been, so was the maiden; modest, gentle and kind, but always earnest and full of life. Surrounding influences naturally guided her busy intellect into inquiries concerning the right principles of human action, and the rationality of customary usages. At seventeen, she professed to have adopted, from her own serious conviction, the religious opinions in which she had been educated. There was little observable change in outward manner; for the fresh spontaneousness of her character had been early chastened by habitual calmness and sobriety. But her views of life gradually became tinged with a larger and deeper thoughtfulness. She often spoke of the freedom of life away from cities, and alone with nature; of mutual helpfulness in such a state of society, and increased means of doing good.

Perhaps her influence, more than anything else, induced her father to purchase a tract of land in New Jersey, with the view of removing thither. Mechanics were sent out to build a suitable house and barns, and the family were to be transplanted to the New World as soon as the necessary arrangements were completed. In the meantime, however, circumstances occurred which led the good man to consider it his duty to remain in England. The younger daughters were well pleased to have it so; but Elizabeth, though she acquiesced cheerfully in her father's decision, evidently had a weight upon her mind. She was more silent than usual, and more frequently retired to her chamber for hours of quiet communion with herself. Sometimes, when asked what she had upon her mind, she replied, in the concise solemn manner of Friends, "It is a great thing to be a humble waiter upon the Lord; to stand in readiness to follow wheresoever He leads the way."

One day, some friends, who were at the house, spoke of the New Jersey tract, and of the reasons which had prevented a removal to America. Her father replied, that he was unwilling to have any property lying useless, and he believed he should offer the tract to any of his relatives who would go and settle upon it. His friends answered, "Thy relatives are too comfortably established in England, to wish to emigrate to the wilds of America."

That evening, when the family were about to separate for the night, Elizabeth begged them to remain a while, as she had something of importance to say. "Dear parents and sisters," said she, "it is now a long time since I have had a strong impression on my mind that it is my duty to go to America. My feelings have been greatly drawn toward the poor brethren and sisters there. It has even been clearly pointed out to me what I am to do. It has been lately signified that a sign would be given when the way was opened; and to-night when I heard thy proposition to give the house and land to whoever would occupy it, I felt at once that thy words were the promised sign."

Her parents, having always taught their children to attend to inward revealings, were afraid to oppose what she so strongly felt to be a duty. Her mother, with a slight trembling in her voice, asked if she had reflected well on all the difficulties of the undertaking, and how arduous a task it was for a young woman to manage a farm of unbroken land in a new country.

Elizabeth replied, "Young women have governed kingdoms; and surely it requires less wisdom to manage a farm. But let not that trouble us, dear mother. He that feedeth the ravens will guide me in the work whereunto he has called me. It is not to cultivate the farm, but to be a friend and physician to the people in that region, that I am called."

Her father answered, "Doubt not, my child, that we shall be willing to give thee up to the Lord's disposings, however hard the trial may be. But when thou wert a very little girl, thy imagination was much excited concerning America; therefore, thou must be very careful that no desire for new adventures, founded in the will of the creature, mislead thee from the true light in this matter. I advise thee for three months to make it a subject of solid meditation and prayer. Then, if our lives be spared, we will talk further concerning it."

During the prescribed time, no allusion was made to the subject, though it was in the thoughts of all; for this highly conscientious family were unwilling to confuse inward perceptions by any expression of feeling or opinion. With simple undoubting faith, they sought merely to ascertain whether the Lord required this sacrifice. That their daughter's views remained the same, they partly judged by her increased tenderness toward all the family. She was not sad, but thoughtful and ever-wakeful, as toward friends from whom she was about to separate. It was likewise observable that she redoubled her diligence in obtaining knowledge of household affairs, of agriculture, and the cure of common diseases. When the three months had expired, she declared that the light shone with undiminished clearness, and she felt, more strongly than ever, that it was her appointed mission to comfort and strengthen the Lord's people in the New World.

Accordingly, early in the spring of 1700, arrangements were made for her departure, and all things were provided that the abundance of wealth, or the ingenuity of affection, could devise. A poor widow of good sense and discretion accompanied her, as friend and housekeeper, and two trusty men servants, members of the Society of Friends. Among the many singular manifestations of strong faith and religious zeal, connected with the settlement of this country, few are more remarkable than the voluntary separation of this girl of eighteen years old from a wealthy home and all the pleasant associations of childhood, to go to a distant and thinly inhabited country, to fulfil what she considered a religious duty. And the humble, self-sacrificing faith of the parents, in giving up their beloved child, with such reverend tenderness for the promptings of her own conscience, has in it something sublimely beautiful, if we look at it in its own pure light. The parting took place with more love than words can express, and yet without a tear on either side. Even during the long and tedious voyage, Elizabeth never wept. She preserved a martyr-like cheerfulness and serenity to the end.

The house prepared for her reception stood in a clearing of the forest, three miles from any other dwelling. She arrived in June, when the landscape was smiling in youthful beauty; and it seemed to her as if the arch of heaven was never before so clear and bright, the carpet of the earth never so verdant. As she sat at her window and saw evening close in upon her in that broad forest home, and heard, for the first time, the mournful notes of the whippo-wil and the harsh scream of the jay in the distant woods, she was oppressed with a sense of vastness, of infinity, which she never before experienced, not even on the ocean. She remained long in prayer, and when she lay down to sleep beside her matron friend, no words were spoken between them. The elder, overcome with fatigue, soon sank into a peaceful slumber; but the young enthusiastic spirit lay long awake, listening to the lone voice of the whippo-wil complaining to the night. Yet notwithstanding this prolonged wakefulness, she rose early and looked out upon the lovely landscape. The rising sun pointed to the tallest trees with his golden finger, and was welcomed with a gush of song from a thousand warblers. The poetry in Elizabeth's soul, repressed by the severe plainness of her education, gushed up like a fountain. She dropped on her knees, and with an outburst of prayer exclaimed fervently, "Oh, Father, very beautiful hast thou made this earth! How bountiful are thy gifts, Lord!"

To a spirit less meek and brave, the darker shades of the picture would have obscured these cheerful gleams; for the situation was lonely and the inconveniences innumerable. But Elizabeth easily triumphed over all obstacles, by her practical good sense and the quick promptings of her ingenuity. She was one of those clear strong natures, who always have a definite aim in view, and who see at once the means best suited to the end. Her first inquiry was, what grain was best adapted to the soil of her farm; and being informed that rye would yield best, "Then I shall eat rye bread," was her answer. The ear of Indian corn, so long treasured in her juvenile museum, had travelled with her across the Atlantic, to be planted in American soil. When she saw fields of this superb plant, she acknowledged that it more than realized the picture of her childish imagination.

But when winter came, and the gleaming snow spread its unbroken silence over hill and plain, was it not dreary then? It would have been dreary indeed to one who entered upon this mode of life from mere love of novelty, or a vain desire to do something extraordinary. But the idea of extended usefulness, which had first lured this remarkable girl into a path so unusual, sustained her through all its trials. She was too busy to be sad, and she leaned too trustingly on her Father's hand to be doubtful of her way. The neighbouring Indians soon loved her as a friend, for they found her always truthful, just, and kind. From their teachings, she added much to her knowledge of simple medicines. So efficient was her skill and so prompt her sympathy, that for many miles round, if man, woman, or child were alarmingly ill, they were sure to send for Elizabeth Haddon; and wherever she went, her observing mind gathered some new hint for the improvement of farm or dairy. Her house and heart were both large; and as her residence was on the way to the Quaker meeting-house in Newtown,[9] it became a place of universal resort to Friends from all parts of the country travelling that road, as well as an asylum for benighted wanderers. When Elizabeth was asked if she were not sometimes afraid of wayfarers, she quietly replied, "Perfect love casteth out fear." And true it was that she, who was so bountiful and kind to all, found none to injure her.

The winter was drawing to a close, when late one evening, the sound of sleigh-bells was heard, and the crunching of snow beneath the hoofs of horses, as they passed into the barn-yard gate. The arrival of travellers was too common an occurrence to excite or disturb the well-ordered family. Elizabeth quietly continued her knitting, merely saying to one of the men, "Joseph, wilt thou put more wood on the fire? These friends, whoever they may be, will doubtless be cold; for I observed at nightfall a chilly feeling, as of more snow in the air."

Great logs were piled in the capacious chimney, and the flames blazed up with a crackling warmth, when two strangers entered. In the younger, Elizabeth instantly recognised John Estaugh, whose preaching had so deeply impressed her at eleven years of age. This was almost like a glimpse of home—her dear old English home! She stepped forward with more than usual cordiality, saying:

"Thou art welcome, Friend Estaugh; the more so for being entirely unexpected."

"And I am glad to see thee, Elizabeth," he replied, with a friendly shake of the hand. "It was not until after I landed in America, that I heard the Lord had called thee hither before me; but I remember thy father told me how often thou hadst played the settler in the woods, when thou wast quite a little girl."

"I am but a child still," she replied, smiling.

"I trust thou art," he rejoined; "and as for these strong impressions in childhood, I have heard of many cases where they seemed to be prophecies sent of the Lord. When I saw thy father in London, I had even then an indistinct idea that I might sometime be sent to America on a religious visit."

"And hast thou forgotten, Friend John, the ear of Indian corn which my father begged of thee for me? I can show it to thee now. Since then I have seen this grain in perfect growth; and a goodly plant it is, I assure thee. See," she continued, pointing to many bunches of ripe corn, which hung in their braided husks against the walls of the ample kitchen: "all that, and more, came from a single ear, no bigger than the one thou didst give my father. May the seed sown by thy ministry be as fruitful!"

"Amen," replied both the guests; and for a few moments no one interrupted the silence. Then they talked much of England. John Estaugh had not seen any of the Haddon family for several years; but he brought letters from them, which came by the same ship, and he had information to give of many whose names were familiar as household words.

The next morning, it was discovered that snow had fallen during the night in heavy drifts, and the roads were impassable. Elizabeth, according to her usual custom, sent out men, oxen and sledges, to open pathways for several poor families, and for households whose inmates were visited by illness. In this duty, John Estaugh and his friend joined heartily, and none of the labourers worked harder than they. When he returned, glowing from this exercise, she could not but observe that the excellent youth had a goodly countenance. It was not physical beauty; for of that he had little. It was that cheerful, child-like, out-beaming honesty of expression, which we not unfrequently see in Germans, who, above all nations, look as if they carried a crystal heart within their manly bosoms.

Two days after, when Elizabeth went to visit her patients, with a sled-load of medicines and provisions, John asked permission to accompany her. There, by the bedside of the aged and the suffering, she saw the clear sincerity of his countenance warmed up with rays of love, while he spoke to them words of kindness and consolation; and there she heard his pleasant voice modulate itself into deeper tenderness of expression, when he took little children in his arms.

The next First Day, which we call the Sabbath, the whole family, as usual, attended Newtown meeting; and there John Estaugh was gifted with an outpouring of the spirit in his ministry, which sank deep into the hearts of those who listened to him. Elizabeth found it so marvellously applicable to the trials and temptations of her own soul, that she almost deemed it was spoken on purpose for her. She said nothing of this, but she pondered upon it deeply. Thus did a few days of united duties make them more thoroughly acquainted with each other, than they could have been by years of fashionable intercourse.

The young preacher soon after bade farewell, to visit other meetings in Pennsylvania and New Jersey. Elizabeth saw him no more until the May following, when he stopped at her house to lodge, with numerous other Friends, on their way to the Quarterly Meeting at Salem. In the morning, quite a cavalcade started from her hospitable door, on horseback; for wagons were then unknown in Jersey. John Estaugh, always kindly in his impulses, busied himself with helping a lame and very ugly old woman, and left his hostess to mount her horse as she could. Most young women would have felt slighted; but in Elizabeth's noble soul the quiet deep tide of feeling rippled with an inward joy. "He is always kindest to the poor and the neglected," thought she; "verily he *is* a good youth." She was leaning over the side of her horse, to adjust the buckle of the girth, when he came up on horseback, and inquired if anything was out of order. She thanked him, with slight confusion of manner, and a voice less calm than her usual utterance. He assisted her to mount, and they trotted along leisurely behind the procession of guests, speaking of the soil and climate of this new country, and how wonderfully the Lord had here provided a home for his chosen people. Presently the girth began to slip, and the saddle turned so much on one side, that Elizabeth was obliged to dismount. It took some time to re-adjust it, and when they again started, the company were out of sight. There was brighter colour than usual in the maiden's cheeks, and unwonted radiance in her mild deep eyes. After a short silence, she said, in a voice slightly tremulous, "Friend John, I have a subject of great importance on my mind, and one which nearly interests thee. I am strongly impressed that the Lord has sent thee to me as a partner for life. I tell thee my impression frankly, but not without calm and deep reflection; for matrimony is a holy relation, and should be entered into with all sobriety. If thou hast no light on the subject, wilt thou gather into the stillness, and reverently listen to thy own inward revealings? Thou art to leave this part of the country to-morrow, and not knowing when I should see thee again, I felt moved to tell thee what lay upon my mind."

The young man was taken by surprise. Though accustomed to that suppression of emotion, which characterizes his religious sect, the colour went and came rapidly in his face, for a moment; but he soon became calmer, and replied, "This thought is new to me, Elizabeth; and I have no light thereon. Thy company has been right pleasant to me, and thy countenance ever reminds me of William Penn's title-page, 'Innocency with her open face.' I have seen thy kindness to the poor, and the wise management of thy household. I have observed, too, that thy warm-heartedness is tempered by a most excellent discretion, and that thy speech is ever sincere. Assuredly, such is the maiden I would ask of the Lord, as a most precious gift; but I never thought of this connexion with thee. I came to this country solely on a religious visit, and it might distract my mind to entertain this subject at present. When I have discharged the duties of my mission, we will speak further."

"It is best so," rejoined the maiden; "but there is one thing disturbs my conscience. Thou hast spoken of my true speech; and yet, Friend John, I have deceived thee a little, even now, while we conferred together on a subject so serious. I know not from what weakness the temptation came; but I will not hide it from thee. I allowed thee to suppose, just now, that I was fastening the girth of my horse securely; but, in plain truth, I was loosening the girth, John, that the saddle might slip, and give me an excuse to fall behind our friends; for I thought thou wouldst be kind enough to come and ask if I needed thy services."

This pure transparency of motive seemed less wonderful to John Estaugh, than it would to a man more accustomed to worldly ways, or less familiar with the simplicity of primitive Quakers. Nevertheless, the perfect guilelessness of the maiden endeared her to his honest heart, and he found it difficult to banish from his thoughts the important subject she had suggested. It was observable in this singular courtship, that no mention was made of worldly substance. John did not say, "I am poor, and thou art rich"; he did not even think of it. And it had entered Elizabeth's mind only in the form of thankfulness to God that she was provided with a home large enough for both.

They spoke no further concerning their union; but when he returned to England, in July, he pressed her hand affectionately, as he said, "Farewell, Elizabeth. If it be the Lord's will, I shall return to thee soon." He lingered, and their hands trembled in each other's clasp; then drawing her gently toward him, he imprinted a kiss on her open innocent forehead. She looked modestly into his clear honest eyes, and replied in the kindest tones, "Farewell, Friend John; may the Lord bless thee and guide thee."

In October, he returned to America, and they were soon after married, at Newtown meeting, according to the simple form of the Society of Friends. Neither of them made any change of dress for the occasion, and there was no wedding feast. Without the aid of priest or magistrate, they took each other by the hand, and, in the presence of witnesses, calmly and solemnly promised to be kind and faithful to each other. Their mutual promises were recorded in the church books, and the wedded pair quietly returned to their happy home, with none to intrude upon those sacred hours of human life, when the heart most needs to be left alone with its own deep emotions.

During the long period of their union, she three times crossed the Atlantic, to visit her aged parents, and he occasionally left her for a season, when called abroad to preach. These temporary separations were felt as a cross, but the strong-hearted woman always cheerfully gave him up to follow his own convictions of duty. In 1742, he parted from her, to go on a religious visit to Tortola, in the West Indies. He died there, in the sixty-seventh year of his age. A friend, in a letter informing her of the event, says: "A shivering fit, followed by fever, seized him on the first day of the tenth month. He took great notice that it ended forty years since his marriage with thee; that during that time you had lived in much love, and had parted in the same; and that leaving thee was his greatest concern of all outward enjoyments. On the sixth day of the tenth month, about six o'clock at night, he went away like a lamb." She published a religious tract of his, to which is prefixed a preface, entitled "Elizabeth Estaugh's testimony concerning her beloved husband, John Estaugh." In this preface, she says, "Since it pleased Divine Providence so highly to favour me, with being the near companion of this dear worthy, I must give some small account of him. Few, if any, in a married state, ever lived in sweeter harmony than we did. He was a pattern of moderation in all things; not lifted up with any enjoyments, nor cast down at disappointments. A man endowed with many good gifts, which rendered him very agreeable to his friends, and much more to me, his wife, to whom his memory is most dear and precious."

Elizabeth survived her excellent husband twenty years, useful and honoured to the last. The Monthly Meeting of Haddonfield, in a published testimonial, speak of her thus: "She was endowed with great natural abilities, which, being sanctified by the spirit of Christ, were much improved; whereby she became qualified to act in the affairs of the church, and was a serviceable member, having been clerk to the women's meeting nearly fifty years, greatly to their satisfaction. She was a sincere sympathiser with the afflicted, of a benevolent disposition, and in distributing to the poor, was desirous to do it in a way most profitable and durable to them, and if possible not to let the right hand know what the left did. Though in a state of affluence as to this world's wealth, she was an example of plainness and moderation. Her heart and house were open to her friends, whom to entertain seemed one of her greatest pleasures. Prudently cheerful, and well knowing the value of friendship, she was careful not to wound it herself, nor to encourage others in whispering supposed failings or weaknesses. Her last illness brought great bodily pain, which she bore with much calmness of mind and sweetness of spirit. She departed this life as one falling asleep, full of days, like unto a shock of corn, fully ripe."

The town of Haddonfield, in New Jersey, took its name from her; and the tradition concerning her courtship is often repeated by some patriarch among the Quakers. She laid out an extensive garden in rear of the house, which during her day was much celebrated for its herbs, vegetables and fruits, liberally distributed all round the neighbourhood. The house was burned down years ago; but some fine old yew trees, which she brought from England, are still pointed out on the site where the noble garden once nourished. Her medical skill is so well remembered, that the old nurses of New-Jersey still recommend Elizabeth Estaugh's salve as the "sovereignest thing on earth."

The brick tomb in which John Estaugh was buried at Tortola, is still pointed out to Quaker travellers; one of whom recently writes, "By a circuitous path, through a dense thicket, we came to the spot where Friends once had a meeting-house, and where are buried the remains of several of our valued ministers, who visited this island about a century ago, from a sense of gospel love. Time has made his ravages upon these mansions of the dead. The acacia spreads thickly its thorny branches over them, and near them the century-blooming aloe is luxuriantly growing."

About the Editor

Sarah Holt is a literature major at Stockton University, with minor concentrations in writing, women, gender and sexuality studies and studio art. She is a musician and a DJ for Stockton's radio station, WLFR.

Endnotes

1. Jeffrey M. Dowart and Elizabeth Lyons, *Elizabeth Haddon Estaugh 1680–1762; Building the Quaker Community of Haddonfield, New Jersey, 1701–1762* (Haddonfield: The Historical Society of Haddonfield, 2013), 5.
2. Dowart et al., *Elizabeth Haddon Estaugh*, 25.
3. Dowart et al., *Elizabeth Haddon Estaugh*, 44.
4. Dowart et al., *Elizabeth Haddon Estaugh*, 77.
5. Dowart et al., *Elizabeth Haddon Estaugh*, 73.
6. Dowart et al., *Elizabeth Haddon Estaugh*, 97.
7. Dowart et al., *Elizabeth Haddon Estaugh*, 22.
8. Dowart et al., *Elizabeth Haddon Estaugh*, 23.
9. The actual meeting was Newton, not Newtown, and it stood along Newton Creek about 10 miles from Elizabeth's house.

Photographer William J. S. Bradway was on-hand to snap an image showing a group of Sunday School excursionists boarding the steamer Clio in August 1906. The steamboat, tied up to the Hancock's Bridge main wharf, was constructed in Wilmington, Delaware, during 1878. She was 94 feet long, 22 feet wide and drew 6 feet of water, allowing her to sail up Alloway Creek, which had a channel 7 feet deep. Her regular route was between Odessa, Delaware, and Philadelphia, carrying both passengers and freight, but management was always ready to earn extra income from the excursion trade. Built to sail smaller tributary streams, owner Frank Watkins sold her to the Rock Creek Steamboat Company of Baltimore in 1908.

The Compendium of New Jersey's Crossroads in Folk Music:
A Q&A with Michael Gabriele

reviewed by Jackson Glassey

In his 2016 *New Jersey Folk Revival Music: History & Tradition*, Michael Gabriele highlights the role that New Jersey—South, North, and everywhere in between—has had in the history of folk music. The New Jersey sound is one that, as Roger Deitz, former trustee of the now-defunct Folk Music Society of Northern New Jersey, proclaims in Part III of the book, "catalyzes" people. Gabriele succeeds in his quest to bring to light the folk music culture in New Jersey. If you consider yourself a connoisseur of folk music, a staunch New Jerseyian with a passion for music history, or just someone curious about folk music as a concept, then this title, published by The History Press of Charleston, South Carolina, is an excellent edition to your library.

Though it clocks in at a lean 190 pages, *New Jersey Folk Revival Music* makes efficient use of its space, packing in a textbook's worth of information relative to its topic, complete with an extensive bibliography and comprehensive index. In his introduction to *Jersey Folk*, Gabriele explains that New Jersey has musical bragging rights beyond those of our state's established stars:

> Ask any stouthearted New Jersey resident about the state's music history and most will proudly list the accomplishments of Frank Sinatra, Count Basie, Bruce Springsteen, Jon Bon Jovi, Bucky Pizzarelli, Dionne Warwick, Leslie Gore, Frankie Valli, Whitney Houston, the Shirelles, Mary Chapin Carpenter, Connie Francis, Sarah Vaughn, Wayne Shorter, the Roches, and many others. The Garden State is acknowledged for its homegrown contributions to pop, rock, and jazz, and rightfully so.
>
> But there's another story to tell: the story of the Garden State's folk revival music heritage. (11)

Over the course of the book's three parts, Gabriele—making use of various interviews, documents, artifacts, illustrations, contributions from private collections, festival reports, and his own photographs—pieces together a wondrous, little-known narrative of New Jersey folk music, one filled with fascinating characters and pivotal locales (Camden's Victor RCA Victor Studios, Rutgers University, Pine Barrens saloons, and the Princeton YMCA are among many scenes set).

I had the pleasure to converse with Mr. Gabriele via email and telephone, and we undertook a question-and-answer session about the book and his experiences writing it. The results of the interview are provided verbatim below.

Q: *To begin, I just want to say that your fascination with folk music and folk revival music comes through clearly in this book. Though it's very academic and intensively researched, I never once doubted that you loved what you were writing about here. Is there a personal history behind your relationship with folk music or music in general? Do you have any memories growing up with music?*

Generally speaking, music has always been part of my life. Today I'm lucky enough to perform, on occasion, at public events and local venues (I'm a sax player). The music I play is typically jazz, blues, and rock. However, I've also taught myself a few guitar chords over the years and enjoying playing with friends at house jams. That stuff gets pretty folky. In fact, just for fun, whenever I get invitations to do talks on my folk music book at libraries and historical societies, I've started bringing along my guitar to perform two or three songs as a folk music sampler.

In the 1960s and 1970s, folk music was always part of the musical mix that I enjoyed—on the radio, at concerts, and on vinyl albums. Folk music wasn't at the top of my list (maybe number three or four), but I enjoyed it.

During the early 1980s, I had a friend who encouraged me to attend a weekly live music venue organized by a group in the Morristown area known as The Folk Project (you'll find this organization mentioned in my book). Attending that venue helped to connect me with the New Jersey folk music circuit. I also enjoy the annual New Jersey Folk Festival at Rutgers.

It's safe to say that attending a live music event at a local venue rates high on my list of preferred social and cultural outings.

Looking back at those days in the 1980s, I certainly enjoyed hearing folk music. I also have great respect for the skill and musicianship of a performer, and I listen to hear their improvisational ideas as they're performing live in front of an audience.

Folk music, in particular, always attracts a nice community of fans—the mingling of the intelligentsia! You meet good people and learn a lot about music and other cultures and regions. It fosters a friendly, warm-hearted atmosphere.

Q: *I thought one of the most interesting points you bring up throughout the book is the important distinction between traditional folk music and revivalist folk music: on a level of traditionalism, folk music serves as a tool for cultural anthropologists and folklorists to study ethnic populations, while folk revivalism focuses more on drawing inspiration from older folk music to create something new and commercially viable. Do you think this is a fitting outlook, or do you believe that, ultimately, folk is folk?*

The distinction between traditional folk and folk revival gets a bit tricky and even controversial. Yes, there's absolutely, positively a distinction between the two; however, I wish people would spend less time arguing about it.

There is certainly a case to be made that traditional folk music is one aspect of cultural anthropology for a given ethnic population and region. And, for academic folklorists, folk music provides an insight on the history of people in a particular time and place. A lot of research work and scholarship goes into the study of folklore as an academic topic. This is an endeavor that deserves to be respected.

The Pineconers playing at the Albert brothers' cabin—the "Homeplace" for folk jams in the Pine Barrens from the mid-1930s to the early 70s, just off Route 532: Janice Sherwood on banjo, Gladys Eayre on rhythm guitar, Joe Albert on washtub (or gut bucket) base, Sammy Hunt on banjo, and George Albert on fiddle. Photograph courtesy of Ted Gordon, September 1972.

NJ Folk Revival Music

Albert Music Hall, Waretown, NJ, constructed in tribute to the Albert Brothers. As of June 2016, this venue has welcomed nearly 300,000 visitors. Photograph courtesy of Michael Gabriele.

But—in terms of our popular culture, the argument about what is or isn't a folk song generally involves the evolution of folk music that was brought to the thirteen colonies in the 1700s. Yes, these are traditional tunes and, in and of themselves, they tell a story about people and history. As I say in the book, this is the music that has been handed down in an oral tradition, generation to generation. These are songs sung by sailors, weavers, and the folks "up in the hills" in parlors and on porches. It's the music of the people.

But this traditional music, especially from England, Ireland, and Scotland, also it is the source that inspired the folk music revival. That's what Cecil Sharp did when he documented traditional tunes from Appalachia and then recorded the songs in Camden. There indeed was a revival of this music; a reassessment, a rediscovery, a re-examination of traditional songs that took on a life of its own.

If you stop and think about it, this isn't anything new. This evolution is quite common in all forms of music. Blues became Rhythm and Blues, which became Rockabilly, which became Rock & Roll, which became Rock, et cetera. The music picks up different sounds, influences, and cultural aspects along the way. Sometimes it's a gradual progression, sometimes is a bit more abrupt—Bob Dylan goes electric at the Newport Folk Festival.

So yes, there's traditional folk, and there's folk revival. That seems pretty clear to me. It's a fair distinction. I think most people, if they stop and think about it, can understand the distinction. And now, folk revival music is evolving into Americana music, progressive folk music, "new grass" music, and so on. The wheels keep turning. So it goes.

My snarky answer to the question concerning what is or isn't folk music? Instead of arguing about it, I'd much rather listen and enjoy all the music.

Q: *I like how the book is organized. Its three parts—"A Silvery Sound: An Unseen Thread," "Revival," and "Jersey Boys (and Girls)"—seem to move through time; starting at riotous colonial-era New Jersey taverns along mail routes; riding towards the nineteenth and twentieth centuries' explosion of recorded audio, gliding along with Jimmie Rodgers at Victor studios, Woody Guthrie's Dust Bowl Ballads RCA sessions, and, of course, Baez and Dylan at the '63 Camden Music Fair; and landing in the present, looking towards to future of New Jersey folk festivals and folk music in general. With that in mind, where do you see folk music in the decades to come? Will it ever have as commercial an appeal as it did back in the 1960s? Will the rise of twenty-first-century indie folk artists like Fleet Foxes and Sun Kil Moon push the genre even further, or will it always be rooted in the vox populi?*

First, thanks for the kind words regarding the structure of the book. Working with my colleagues at The History Press, we put a lot of thought into the organization and flow of the narrative, so I appreciate that you noticed. Regarding the direction of folk music in the decades to come—it's always difficult to try and predict how the future will unfold. As Yogi Berra once said: "The future ain't what it used to be." However, a few things do come to mind. Based on what I see at New Jersey music festivals, as well as what I'm told by trusted sources, I'd say the folk revival scene will continue to attract musicians that have a strong "indie" spirit. I think you'll see this independent spirit in the music they produce and perform; you'll also see it in how they conduct business and manage their careers. Because of digital technology, many artists enjoy the freedom of producing and distributing their own music. As for the music itself, nothing will ever replace the magical sound of skillfully played acoustic instruments (guitar, mandolin, banjo, fiddle, upright bass, etc.) and dazzling vocal harmonies. You will see other instruments added to the mix. Folk music, by definition and tradition, will remain rooted as the music of the people; the poetry, subject matter, and styles of performing continue to evolve. Artists are always taking traditional sounds and styles, and moving them into new directions. I applaud that. New artists will keep moving forward to create beautiful new music. No worries.

Q: *Is there a particular portion of the book you found extra compelling to write and research? Did you find that focusing specifically on New Jersey's role in the rise of folk music made writing the book more interesting and engaging overall, that it gave you an edge over other books about folk music?*

I've written three books for my publisher, The History Press, and they're all about New Jersey history. I stay within the friendly confines of the Garden State. My angle as an author is always focused on New Jersey. I see that as an advantage, compared with other books that cover a more general subject matter. I can drill down and explore specific people, places, and events in detail. New Jersey is a never-ending source of inspiration with a long, colorful history. As a lifelong Jersey guy, it's meaningful to me. There's a strong local audience for local history. That's the audience I'm aiming to reach.

The second chapter, "Revival," was especially compelling in terms of writing and research. I enjoyed uncovering important events that took place in New Jersey, like the early Camden recording sessions. I also learned about how New Jersey became an important part of the musical journeys of people like Paul Robeson, Joan Baez, Woody Guthrie, Josh White, Bob Dylan, and Pete Seeger.

New Jersey Folk Revival Music: History & Tradition is available for purchase from Arcadia Publishing, Amazon, and all major book retail outlets. Published by The History Press, 2016.

About the Reviewer

Jackson Glassey is a Literature major at Stockton University in his senior year. He is President of the Literature Club, a managing editor for *Stockpot* (Stockton's annual literary magazine), and a regular contributor to Stockton's weekly newspaper, *The Argo*. More of his writing can be found on his music blog, The Music Zealot (themusiczealot.com).

Musicians at the 2015 New Jersey Folk Festival. Photograph courtesy of Michael Gabriele.

The Bayshore Center:
A Unique Maritime Experience on the Delaware Bay

Jessica English

The Bayshore Center at Bivalve is one of South Jersey's hidden gems. Located alongside the Maurice River, the center consists of seven refurbished oyster shipping sheds and their attached covered wharves, all of which have been restored to look like they have not aged beyond the 1920s, which were glory days of oystering in the Delaware Bay. As home to both the Delaware Bay Museum and the retired oyster schooner A. J. Meerwald, New Jersey's official state tall ship, the Bayshore Center is an important historical and cultural venue in South Jersey.

The museum, which occupies several of the restored oyster sheds, offers an intimate look into New Jersey's historic and once-prolific oyster industry. Photos and artifacts, including small boats, pieces of old ship rigging, and oyster processing equipment, are exhibited in functional and meaningful ways. An interactive model of an oyster processing unit partially occupies a shed, while the second story of another shed features a replica of an oysterman's office. Historical accounts from oyster shuckers and the crew of the oyster boats are peppered throughout the displays, providing a personal touch to the exhibits. A gift shop and a café also occupy part of the sheds.

The A. J. Meerwald sailing on open water.

The A. J. Meerwald is at once an exhibit and an extension of the museum. The 90-year-old schooner has a long and tumultuous history, beginning with its 1928 commissioning by brothers Augustus C. "Gus" and William "Bill" Meerwald. Less than a decade later, the brothers fell on hard times during the Great Depression, with Gus losing his home in the process. As the brothers began to get back onto their feet in the early 1940s, World War II broke out, and the federal Maritime Commission commandeered the A. J. Meerwald to be used by the U. S. Coast Guard as a fireboat on the Delaware River during the war. The ship survived its brief stint as a military vessel, but over the next several years, the schooner changed hands several times and was renamed the Clyde A. Phillips. From the late 1950s until being retired in 1978, the vessel was converted to harvest surf clams. Starting in 1979, the ship stood idle for nearly a decade, before sinking in the Maurice River in 1988, due to neglect. Twenty-three-year-old Meghan Wren of Millville had a vision for the schooner, assembled the community, raised $800,000, and, with both a full-time restoration crew and a group of dedicated volunteers, restored the schooner to its former beauty and christened it the A. J. Meerwald once again.

A scale model of an oyster schooner.

The A. J. Meerwald during its time as a Coast Guard fireboat.

A recreated oyster processing unit.

Cape May Salt and Elder Point Oysters, next to the Bayshore Center. Bivalve is still a working waterfront.

Bayman's Office Display.

The Bayshore Center

The schooner remains in operation today, though not as an oystering vessel. It serves as an educational vehicle, as well as providing the opportunity for leisurely public sails. School groups are welcome to come aboard and learn about history and the environment, both when it is docked in the Bayshore Center and when it is at port at various locations along the New Jersey coastline. The ship is also available for public and corporate charters.

While preservation of the past is a central goal at the Bayshore Center, preservation of the present is arguably more important to those working at the center. The oystering industry has experienced several severe downturns over the past century due to overfishing and environmental changes, including human-generated pollution and the introduction of two parasitic diseases that killed off more than 90% of the oysters in 1957 and again in 1990. Facing the devastation that man-made environmental instability caused their livelihood, South Jersey oystermen felt the need to take responsible action to become better stewards of their environment and to protect their way of life, ensuring future generations' security.

The desire to conserve the local environment and to harvest oysters in a sustainable manner have become touchstones for New Jersey oystermen and the Bayshore Center. In 2002, the Bayshore Center at Bivalve partnered with the Cumberland County Improvement Authority to build a floating dock out of recycled plastic, preventing nearly 240,000 plastic milk jugs from being unsustainably disposed of, and much of the curriculum offered aboard the A. J. Meerwald centers on environmental sustainability. All proceeds from food at the Oyster Cracker Café, the Bayshore Center's in-house restaurant, go towards the environmental educational programming.

The Bayshore Center offices are open Monday through Friday, 9 am – 4:30 pm and the Delaware Bay Museum is open Wednesday through Sunday, 11 am – 3 pm, April through October. They are located at 2800 High Street, Port Norris, New Jersey, 08349. The Meerwald sails April through October and, during the winter months, the center remains available for group tours and programs. The center's library and archives are open for research by appointment. If you have questions about purchasing sail tickets, charters, donating to the Bayshore Center, or visiting the museum, call (856)–785-2060 or email Info@BayshoreCenter.org.

About the Author

Jessica English is a literature major at Stockton University in the creative writing track.

(Above) A life ring on the dock at the Bayshore Center.
(Below) The landward side of the Bayshore Center.

SoJourn
Call for Articles

The South Jersey Culture & History Center at Stockton University publishes twice yearly issues of *SoJourn*. We actively seek community members, avocational historians, and scholars to contribute essays on topics related to South Jersey. Illustrations to accompany these articles will be a plus. Articles should be written for laypersons who are interested and curious about South Jersey topics, but do not necessarily have expertise in the areas covered. Potential authors should check SJCHC's website for a link to a simplified style sheet guide for article preparation—www.stockton.edu/sjchc/—or just follow the style in this issue. Journal editors will be happy to guide any would-be authors. In certain instances, Stockton editing interns may be assigned to help research topics and/or assist authors with writing.

Sample topics might include:
Biographical sketches of important but forgotten local people; the development or succession of a community's roads, bridges or buildings; local transportation (focused by mode, area or era) and what changes it wrought in the served communities; history of community businesses and industries (wineries, garment factories, agriculture, boat building, clamming, etc.); old school houses, old hotels, or meeting halls; narrative descriptions of local geographical features; essays concerned with folklore, music, arts; and reviews of new local interest publications. Photo essays and old photograph and postcard reproductions are welcome with applicable captions. In short, if a South Jersey topic interests you, it will likely interest *SoJourn*'s readers.

Parameters for submissions:
• Submissions must pertain to topics bounded within the eight southernmost counties of New Jersey (Burlington & Ocean Counties and south)
• Manuscripts should be approximately 3,000–4,000 words long (5 to 7 pages of single-spaced text and 9 to 12 pages including images)
• Manuscripts should conform to the *SoJourn* style sheet, available here:
https://blogs.stockton.edu/sjchc/sojourn-style-sheet/
• Manuscripts, if at all possible, should be submitted in digital format (Word- or pdf-formatted documents preferred)
• Images should be submitted as high-resolution tiff- or jpeg-formatted files (editors can assist with digital conversion of photos if necessary). 300 dpi resolution, or higher, preferred
• Complete and appropriate citations printed as endnotes should be employed (see style sheet). If using Word, please use its endnote function
• Original submissions only. Copyright licenses for all images must be obtained by the author or should be copyright-free figures and/or figures in the public domain
• If essays are accepted, authors should submit a short 50 to 100 word autobiographical statement
• Articles need to be more than just a chronology of the given topic. The author should be able to properly contextualize the subject by answering such questions as: a) why is this important?; b) what is the impact on the local or regional history? and c) how does it compare to similar events/personages/changes/processes in other localities?

Call for submissions:
Submissions for winter issues are due before September 1; for summer issues, January 15.

Send inquiries or submissions to Thomas.Kinsella@stockton.edu or Paul.Schopp@stockton.edu.

This happy couple standing on the beach in their bathing suits with the magnificent Marlborough-Blenheim Hotel in the background, is Jennie Stauffer and Roy Keen, as noted on the postcard. They probably visited Atlantic City during the summer of 1910, since they wedded on September 17 of that same year. Roy and Jennie resided in Spring City, Chester County, Pennsylvania, where Roy worked as a house painter and paperhanger. The couple had three daughters. Roy died in 1963 and Jennie passed in 1976.

REAR COVER

Left to Right, Top Row:

Pennsauken: The Pensauken (sic) School stood at the corner of Park and Cooper avenues. As the student population grew, so did the school during the second half of the nineteenth century. Designated as School no. 5, the building remained in service until 1911, when the school board constructed a new brick school on Union Avenue. School officials sold the old no. 5 to a Mr. Rudderow, who divided the building and made the three sections into three houses proximate to the former school yard.

Cologne: Beginning in the mid-nineteenth century, Germans emigrated the lands belonging to the Gloucester Farm and Town Association. Small rural hamlets nucleated around farm produce shipping points along the Camden & Atlantic Railroad. These rural communities included Cologne, Germania, and Pomona and all three had schools for the farm children to attend. This view shows the first school in Cologne, constructed sometime during the second half of the nineteenth century.

Left to Right, Second Row:

Robbinsville, Port Norris: Located along Main Street at Lincoln Street in Port Norris, the Robbinstown School dates to 1856, when it initially served as a house of worship for two denominations before it became a public school in 1867. The school closed in the late 1960s then reopened for special education classes through 1977. Twenty years later, a group of concerned citizens acquired the building from the school board, rehabilitated it, and opened a library and museum in October 1997.

Berlin: This 1874 two-story frame schoolhouse replaced two one-room schools in Berlin, formerly Long-A-Coming. The new building featured three classrooms and stood on Main Street near the municipal offices, one of the old schools. By 1886, 142 students attended the school, but it became obsolete by 1914. School officials erected a new brick school in front of the frame building and the 1874 structure was razed a few years later.

Left to Right, Third Row:

Holly Beach: Built in 1886, the Holly Beach Public School stood between New Jersey and Pacific avenues and Andrews and Burk avenues on Five Mile Beach. The school continued educating successive generations of children until 1933, when the local school board closed it. Three years later, the building was razed. Three years later, Holly Beach Park opened on the land formerly hosting the school. The park features the old school bell, a fountain, and memorial to fishermen.

Hartford School, Shamong: In 1805, the Upper Evesham Quaker Preparatory Meeting purchased three acres at Brotherton to establish a school and burial ground. A year later, the Hartford School opened for students. Sometime after 1840, it became a public school. In 1905, the local school board built a replacement building. Three years later, the board sold the old Hartford School to Thomas Gardner for $87.55, who removed it from the lot to his own property.

Oceanville no. 4: The students have assembled on the steps of Galloway Township School no. 4 in Oceanville for photographer Max H. Kirscht to snap a photograph. Although a definitive date could not be found for this school, its design suggests its construction occurred during the 1860s. The carriage on the right side of the photograph belonged to the photographer.

Left to Right, Fourth Row:

Pennsgrove: Long known as the "Eight Square School," this octagon single-story brick structure stood almost three miles above Penns Grove along Crown Point Road in the area that became Camp Pederick during the First World War. The marble lintel over the main door featured "Pennsgrove" incised into it.

Mount Holly: Constructed at the corner of Brainerd and Buttonwood streets in 1893, this large brick grade school continued to serve Mount Holly students until 1962, when the Holbein School opened on Levis Drive. Attempts by various organization to purchase the old school failed and the school board awarded a demolition contract to Harry J. Alloway at a cost of $5,090 in late 1962. Today, the property is part of the Woolman Commons division of Medford Leas.